THE GOSPEL
OF THE TOLTECS

THE GOSPEL
OF THE
TOLTECS

THE LIFE

AND

TEACHINGS

OF

QUETZALCOATL

Frank Díaz

Translated by Luix Saldaño

Foreword by Victor Sanchez

Bear & Company
Rochester, Vermont

Bear & Company
One Park Street
Rochester, Vermont 05767
www.InnerTraditions.com

Bear & Company is a division of Inner Traditions International
Copyright © 2002 by Frank Díaz

LIBRARY OF CONGRESS CATALOGING-IN-PUBLICATION DATA
Díaz, Frank, 1964–
[Evangelio de Quetzalcoatl. English]
The gospel of the Toltecs : the life and teachings of Quetzalcoatl / Frank Díaz ;
foreword by Victor Sanchez ; translated by Luix Saldaño.
p. cm.
Includes bibliographical references.
ISBN 978-1-879181-86-1 (pbk.)
1. Spiritual life. 2. Toltecs—Religion—Miscellanea. 3. Quetzalcoatl (Aztec
deity)—Miscellanea. I. Title.
BL624.D58513 2002
299'.792—dc21
2002005006

Printed and bound in the United States

10   9   8   7   6   5   4   3   2

Text design and layout by Virginia Scott Bowman
This book was typeset in Sabon with Mesozoic Gothic and Lucida Sans
as the display typefaces
Chapter opening illustrations are from Codex Laud, facsimile edition
(Austria: Editorial Graz, 1966)

CONTENTS

PART TWO

FOREWORD

WHEN I WAS A BOY going to elementary school in México, I heard about the Toltec for the first time. They were an indigenous people from the times before the Spanish conquest and were, I was told, one of the more important ethnic groups from our historical past. I learned that they lived between the eighth and twelfth century C.E., disappearing from the face of the earth three hundred years before the Spanish arrived in México in 1521.

I didn't know then that the Toltec were going to play such a large part in my development as an adult and a key role in my career. As my life developed, I made two major findings related to the Toltec that I hadn't anticipated in my years of elementary school. The first one occured during my explorations of the wilderness in Mexico. I used to go on long walks in the countryside and while doing so I came to know the people of many indigenous communities. Among them I discovered those whom I call the surviving Toltec—indigenous people who, at the beginning of the twentieth century, are keeping alive the spiritual tradition of the ancient Toltec.

The second unexpected occurrence was finding, in the 1990s, that the Toltec were becoming a topic of great interest to spiritual seekers in the United States and Europe.

Interestingly, while there have been offered on the spiritual scene many books, lectures, and even workshops around topics related to the Toltec, there has been very little information about the real Toltec, namely the historical Toltec and the surviving Toltec. In other words, most of what is said about them comes from the elaboration of authors who use the word *Toltec* to label or frame their own proposals for personal or spiritual development.

I can see that the result of this liberal association with the Toltec usually brings benefits to those using these books, lectures, and workshops to inspire their growth process. But there is another side to this: Because of the disconnect between the presentation of Toltec topics and actual historical and field research, modern spiritual seekers are getting to know the real Toltec wisdom that resides in both the actual indigenous communities and in historical sources.

A good example of this is that, while many people are familiar with the word *Toltec*, very few people are familiar with the most important Toltec spiritual leader, Ce Acatl Topiltzin, or Quetzalcoatl. He was an extraordinary human being whose role for the Toltec and Maya was similar to that of Jesus Christ for the Christians, Buddha for the Buddhists, or Muhammad for the Muslims.

In my own field, I have tried to contribute to the task of bringing a deeper understanding of Toltec wisdom by reporting my experiences with the surviving Toltec (see *Toltecs of the New Millennium,* Santa Fe: Bear and Company, 1996), which have come from my field research. It is in this context of illuminating Toltec wisdom that the research of Frank Díaz on the historical Toltec—and especially on their spiritual leader, Quetzalcoatl—is so relevant.

His work comes to fill an enormous gap in our understanding of the Toltec, and in this *The Gospel of the Toltecs,* which recounts the life and teachings of Quetzalcoatl, is a huge achievement. Díaz immersed himself in codices from the sixteenth and seventeenth centuries, deciphered the meaning of the glyphs, made the linguistic transcription of the text from Nahuatl (the language of the Toltec and Aztec), and put it all together in such a way that every reader may understand and benefit from it.

The history of Quetzalcoatl is the story of a spiritual person struggling to give a deeper meaning to his life and the life of his people. It is the story of a person who must face temptation, failure, and a fall, and then must stand up again and continue his sacred task. We may see in his story the reflection of our own duality. We are looking for God, yes, but we have to do it carrying with us both our virtues and our weaknesses. That is the essence of our duality, the duality that is represented by the Toltec symbol of Quetzalcoatl— the feathered serpent, the union of that which crawls and that which flies. *The Gospel of the Toltecs* is relevant, then, not only for those interested in the Toltec and for those interested in spiritual traditions, but also for those pursuing their own personal growth.

There is still so much to be discovered in the ancient codices, much that is waiting to be deciphered and translated. Until they are revealed in full, we have the work of Frank Díaz to help us discover the real roots of one of the most extraordinary and profound spiritual traditions of humanity: the Toltequity.

VICTOR SANCHEZ

PART ONE

Our parents and grandparents tell us that
He created us, He, whose creation we are:
Our lord Quetzalcoatl.
He also created the heavens, the sun,
and the divine earth.

CHAPTER ONE
PROPHECY OF HUEMAN THE ELDER

1 Year Ten Calli (33 B.C.E.).[1] I want to talk to you of Hueman the Elder, astrologer and prophet who lived many centuries ago; who, being almost three hundred years of age, felt that death was coming. He then gathered all the Toltec stories existing since the creation of the world, and had these written in a book where he recorded all of his work and prosperity, the life of kings, their laws and good government.

2 He wrote all the axioms of the ancient knowledge, the metaphors and the philosophy, and recorded all the astrological knowledge, architectural data, and secret arts of his time. After summarizing everything, he sealed the book and branded it *Teomoxtli.*[2]

3 Hueman predicted that one millennium after his death,[3] with the acquiescence of some and against the will of others, a lord would rise to the throne; and that he would carry certain signs on his body, the main one being an abundance of hair with which nature would shape a crown around his head, from the time he exited his mother's womb until his death; and that he would have a beard and would resemble a god.

4 He also prophesied Quetzalcoatl's life conduct, which at the beginning would be just and wise, then, as he reached middle age, would be stubborn and unfortunate. Because of this, his nation would suffer great punishment from the heavens and certain priests would rise up against him, all of which would make him flee to the south. After the manifestation of this sign, the destruction of the Toltecs would begin.

5 At that time the women of higher status would give themselves to carnal excesses, and in the temples the priests would break from their obligations and deliver themselves to quarreling and idolatry, and they would come to shed human blood on the altars. Because of all of this, the irate Earth would deny them sustenance and would throw them far away. She would punish them with lightning, frost, hail, and fire, and would instigate war among themselves, with which they would annihilate each other.

6 After all this, Quetzalcoatl would return as a god from his travels, and as such he would be recognized by everyone. Thanks to his knowledge of the *Tonalamatl,*[4] Hueman came to know all of this. And with time, everything came to pass through divine will.

Source for this chapter: *Relaciones históricas.*

1. This date corresponds to the Nahuatl system. Only the dates that have been ver-
   ified will appear at chapter openings throughout the text.
2. Translates as "divine book."
3. The word *millennium* expresses the sense of the Nahuatl term *Huey Xiuhpo-
   hualli*, or "great knotting of the years." This seems to have been the calendar
   time assigned for all of Quetzalcoatl's returns.
4. *Book of the Days:* an astrology handbook used by Mesoamerican priests.

CHAPTER TWO

CHIMALMA

1 Year Ten Tecpatl (930 C.E.). By the town of Amatlan[1] in a house called Pochotitla,[2] there lived a childless elderly couple. Daily they would plead to Ometeotl[3] that they could raise a child. The old man's name was Cipactonal. The old woman's name was Oxomoc.[4] He was a priest and she was a priestess, both for the temple of Tlamanco.

2 In due time Ometeotl gave them a baby daughter whom they baptized as Chimalma.[5] After the birth, Oxomoc dreamed of Tlaloc's[6] sons: In the dream, they predicted that her daughter would not marry; however, she would give birth to a boy. To avoid such a disgrace, they educated Chimalma with much modesty and discretion.

3 Then she grew up and instead of occupying herself with feminine labor, she started to learn the use of weapons. Many neighbors came to ask her hand in marriage, but to her parents' sorrow, she refused to marry. She would only train for war. In this manner, time passed and Chimalma turned seventeen. She was a young maiden of beautiful appearance.

 Source for this chapter: *Leyenda del Tepozteco.*

1. "Place of codices." Ancient place located between the actual towns of Tepoztlan, Santo Domingo Ocotitlan, and Amatlan de Quetzalcoatl.
2. "Among the ceibas." Its ruins can be found in the valley of Xomolco, in Amatlan de Quetzalcoatl.
3. "Divine dual trinity." Nahuatl name for the Supreme Being. From the roots *om,* "two"; *e,* "three"; and *teo,* "divine."
4. Cipactonal, "light of the dragon," and Oxomoc, a name without translation in the Nahuatl language and originating from the Mayan name Xmucane, "the great-grandmother," are mythological entities, the original creators of the fifth human race.
5. "Shield in hand." A nickname that she was given because of her warrior's profession, and also because she represented the lunar goddess.
6. This name can be translated as "all over the earth" and also as "the thundering one." It also refers to Ometeotl's shape as the deity of the storms.

CHAPTER THREE
THE DEER

1 Year Ten Acatl (943 C.E.). Around that time there was a great noise in the sky and a two-headed deer fell down to earth.[1] A man named Mixcoatl,[2] who was a hunter in the valley of Anahuac, chased it with the intention of putting an arrow through it. For one night and one day he went after the deer until he caught it.

2 He then sent the deer to the people of his town, ordering them to nurture it from then on as an Ometeotl omen. They did as they were told. They fed the deer for four years, offering him rabbits and butterflies. But the deer died. They then took the skin and raised it as a flag.

3 After this time there was a war. Mixcoatl took the skin of the deer and leading to combat some of the people from the region, carried them to victory. Then, with the intention of taking prisoners, he went to a place named Comalcan. When the inhabitants learned of this, they came to greet him, offering tribute and honors.

4 He then went to the city of Tecoma, where he was similarly received. They there said to him: "What are you doing, Lord? Be welcome!" He then ordered: "Go and bring me the corncob! In this place I will shell it." Once the ceremony was completed, promptly the people of Tecoma named him their king.

5 City after city, people would submit to him. Everywhere he rose up with victory. And the skin of the deer was his shield. And that is how under his leadership the kingdom of the Toltecs was unified.[3]

🌀 Source for this chapter: *Anales de Cuautitlán.*

---

1. The deer is the symbol of the sun. His forked antlers represent nature's evolution. This episode alludes to the coming of the Fifth Sun or the Toltec Age.
2. "Serpent of clouds." Incarnation of the sun and the Milky Way; god of the fire.
3. The unification of the Toltec kingdom lasted two centuries, until just before Ce Acatl was born. Here Mixcoatl represents the entire dynasty of Toltec kings. Also, as we will see, he represents the fecund force of Ometeotl. His calendar name, Ce Tecpatl, "one stone," shows that he was also seen as an incarnation of the dark shape of the Supreme Being, called Tezcatlipoca, "smoking mirror."

CHAPTER FOUR
IN THE RAVINE

1 Year Thirteen Tochtli (946 C.E.). In order to conquer the place, Mixcoatl arrived at the outskirts of Amatlan. The town elders met and told themselves: "Look! Thanks to his banner he is triumphant; the deerskin is powerful! Let's take it away from him!" To carry on with such a purpose, they decided to send an able warrior to meet and subdue him.

2 One night, all by himself, Mixcoatl took to the road to spy around the town. He hid in a ravine named Huitznahuac,[1] in a hut made of branches that was built specifically for protection, and there he spent the night.

3 Early in the morning, according to her custom, young Chimalma came to bathe in the ravine. With bow, shield, and arrows she was dressed and equipped for war. When she reached the water, she dropped her weapons and her clothes, and there she stood naked.

4 At that very moment Mixcoatl woke up and he saw her, then took his bow and tried to put an arrow through her. Four times he shot at her. But the young one was skillful and avoided his arrows. On the first try, she just tilted her head and the arrow did not touch her; on the second try, the arrow came directly to her waist but she just moved her hip. The third arrow she simply caught with her hand; and the fourth one went between her legs.[2]

5 Seeing this, Mixcoatl returned to his hut to get more arrows. But immediately Chimalma ran away and hid in a cave deep in the ravine. Mixcoatl came back and searched for her but did not find her. As a result of this he felt aggravated and so went to Amatlan and took everyone prisoner.

6 Then the elders said to themselves: "Let's deliver the woman Chimalma!" So they sent a message to the cave where she was hiding, saying: "Mixcoatl the warrior wants to see you; because you ran away he is keeping your younger brothers hostages and is mistreating your sisters.[3] We beg you to return." Therefore she returned.

7 Then the king took her and sent her to a temple in the place called Tlamanco. His orders were that she should not receive any visitors; nor was she to go out. Only then was his rage diminished.

8 Back in Amatlan he gathered the elders and made them swear loyalty to the Toltec kingdom. He then established a tribute. He also committed them to guard Chimalma's virginity until his return, when he would take her as his wife. Then he went back to his home in Tula.

9 Regarding the deerskin, seeing that it was a cause for dispute, he burned it, and while it was on fire it exploded several times and sent out colored stone chips. With the first explosion, stones of celestial blue flew out; with the second, a white stone came out; the third time, red and yellow pebbles; and last, a black stone similar to obsidian flew off the fire. Mixcoatl then took the white stone and worshiped it in memory of the goddess of that place, whose name was Itzpapalotl.[4]

✳ Source for this chapter: *Anales de Cuautitlán.*

---

1. "Among the thorns." Possible archaic name of the canyon today named Xochi-atlahco, between Amatlan de Quetzalcoatl and Yauhtepec.
2. This episode with a clearly erotic resonance represents the virgin's impregnation by the solar spirit.
3. These individuals have direct correspondences to astronomical bodies: Mixcoatl is the sun, Chimalma is the moon, and her brothers and sisters represent the stars.
4. "Obsidian butterfly." This deity represents the incarnation and the human birth. *Itz,* "stone," is the body, while *papalotl,* "butterfly," is the immortal soul.

CHAPTER FIVE
THE SOOTHSAYER FISH

1 Year Thirteen Tochtli (946 C.E.). Chimalma used to do her penitence in the Tlamanco Temple. Every morning she would bathe in a very beautiful cave located at the foot of a mountain, inside of which there was a fountain of pure waters.

2 Once, as she finished her bath, she sat at the water's edge and there she observed something shining in the pond. She tried to take it, but a fish came forth, lifting his head out of the water to present her with an object, a jade bead.[1] After this occurrence, that place was called Michintlauhco.[2]

3 Chimalma took the bead, and to keep it safe she put it under her tongue. But while she was returning to her chores, she accidentally swallowed it, and from this she became pregnant.

✽ Source for this chapter: *Leyenda del Tepozteco.*

1. In Mesoamerica, jade had the highest value and therefore represented the divine fertile spirit.
2. "The canyon of the fish." At present this place is called Michatlahco. The fish as a symbol representing the Savior appears in a number of spiritual traditions of the world.

CHAPTER SIX

THE ORACLE

1 After a time, the first symptoms of Chimalma's pregnancy started to become apparent. When Mixcoatl was notified of this he became very angry and exclaimed, "If she has been stained, she deserves death." Therefore, he decided to consult with the diviners to learn the reality of the matter.

2 The officials threw the charms and the oracle told them how young Chimalma became pregnant. Then he added: "Tell Mixcoatl it is important that he take care of the woman and her son, for the essence of heaven has come down to earth, the spirit of grace has manifested itself. Her son will break and drill the back of the mountains."

3 When the diviners heard the answer they got scared, and they counseled the king in concordance with the oracle. He then ordered that young Chimalma be sent to her parents' house in Amatlan where she would be cared for until the birth of her son.

4 Additionally, he came out publicly to announce his wedding with Chimalma and he recognized the child as his own. But this news angered his brothers, the princes Zolton and Cuilton.[1] Therefore, they decided to kill the king and take his son as soon as he was born.

⬡ Sources for this chapter: *Anales de Cuautitlán* and *Relaciones históricas.*

---

1. "Eater" and "usurper." They are not historical figures, but they represent the incarnation of the negative forces that provoked the Toltecs' downfall.

CHAPTER SEVEN
THE BIRTH

1 Year One Acatl (947 C.E.). Zolton and Cuilton hired some foreign warriors with the intention of having them ambush and kill Mixcoatl. On a certain day, while the king was walking by the sea, he was attacked and slain. After that, the warriors hid his body in the sand. The king was thirty-nine years old.

2 Zolton and Cuilton came to power in Mixcoatl's place, promising the people they would reign until the king's child became an adult. Meanwhile, they hired certain midwives first to assist Chimalma in the birth and then to kill the newborn child.

3 When the midwives arrived in the town of Amatlan, they informed Chimalma: "Alas, your husband has been assassinated and we have come to assist you in your pain."

4 On hearing such news, the child moved within Chimalma and birth pains came to her. Making haste the midwives prepared a bed and everything else that was needed. But Chimalma asked to be taken to the cave of the soothsayer fish to give birth.

5 Then they dressed her like a queen, with turquoise adornments. They sat her upon a hand chair with a seat made from a turtle shell. In her hand they placed the symbol of royalty. And they took her to the cave.[1]

6 That is how Chimalama gave birth with all of her ensigns in attendance. She endured a great deal of pain. For four days she struggled to have her child until, raising her voice, she screamed: "Rise up now, be sent, you new child, you jewel child. Rise up, be done with!" Saying all this, she gave birth, then immediately died.

✳ Sources for this chapter: *Anales de Cuautitlán* and *Romances de los señores de la Nueva España.*

---

1. The birth of an avatar in a cave is a universal theme in the world's spiritual traditions. The site of this birth can still be found in the ravine of Michatlahco, but the cave's entrance remains hidden.

CHAPTER EIGHT

EHECAPILTONTLI

1 To fulfill their mission, the midwives took the child on a shield to an agave plant and threw him on it so that its needles would pierce him. The next morning they came back to get the body, but they found instead a smiling child. The agave had fed the child with its honey throughout the night.[1]

2 Then the midwives threw him on an anthill. Later, assuming the child was dead, they returned a second time. But the child was still alive. The ants had placed him on a flowerbed and had fed him corn porridge.[2]

3 A third time they threw him in a spring to be drowned in its water. Its current dragged him and carried him far. Then the midwives told themselves: "Now he is dead, indeed he is!" And they went back to Tula to give the princes the news.[3]

4 But the child did not die. His body floated on the surface of the water while the current took him along and sweetly delivered him to the sand. By chance a wood gatherer, a native of the town of Yauhtepec, was passing by on his way to sell his wood in the town of Amatlan. Seeing the small body, he picked him up and took him to his town where he showed him to the elders.

5 When Cipactonal had been informed by the midwives that his daughter and grandson had died, he was overcome by great sorrow. But on seeing the child that the wood gatherer was carrying, it became clear to him that this was Chimalma's son. He then dropped to the ground and worshiped the goddess of that place, Itzpapalotl.

6 And because of the child's portentous survival, his grandfather named him Ehecapiltontli.[4] But being born in a Ce Acatl year, this became his calendar nickname, and with great secrecy he was educated to be the heir of Pochotitla.

7 Such is the way the elders tell of Ce Acatl's birth, and such is the way it happened. But in reality he was not just born, but rather came back. He came to manifest himself there in that place.[5] From where did he come? And where did he go? Nobody knows for certain, only Ipalnemohuani.[6]

(❁) Sources for this chapter: *Leyenda del Tepozteco* and *Romances de los señores de la Nueva España.*

---

1. The agave represents Mayahuel, the god of ritual drunkenness, who is the feminine counterpart of Tezcatlipoca.
2. The ant is another symbol for Quetzalcoatl because of her peculiar way of opening tunnels, her labor, and her association with seeds. As a black ant, Quetzacoatl

traveled to the core of the earth to get the sacred seeds of corn in order to create the humanity of the Fifth Sun.

3. The water spring is another frequently used messianic symbol. Quetzalcoatl is considered to be the human form of Tlaloc, the god of water.

4. "Sun of the wind" or "little prince of the spirit."

5. This expression underlines the belief in a periodic return of the avatar.

6. "The one for whom we live" is another name for the Supreme Being.

CHAPTER NINE

CHILDHOOD

1 The child was brought up under the guidance of his grandparents. He was quick to grow and was very precocious and could skillfully handle a bow. With great accuracy he would hunt with arrows of his own making. On his seventh birthday Cipactonal presented him with the inheritance of his mother's weapons.

2 Frequently he would leave home, traveling deep into the ravine, and not return until dusk. His grandparents would reprimand him, but he would say nothing, he would only listen. But once he responded: "Parents of mine, please do not worry. I only go hunting through the ravine and in the mountains. I always take with me the arrows and the bow that mother made for me, and the arrows have a point of stone. Do not be restless."

3 And they asked him what he was really doing in the cliffs and the ravine. Then he answered: "I am going to bring down the divine one of the antlers, because our lives are waiting for him. I am going to track him down wherever he is, be it on the cliffs, on the slopes, or in the mountains. I will bring you his meat and feed you."[1]

4 But his grandparents did not want to believe him, so again they started to reprimand him. Then Ce Acatl took his bow, shot an arrow behind himself without looking, and pierced a deer. When the elders saw this they grew very scared, and they told themselves: "In truth we know nothing of this child. Where did he come from? Why is he the way that he is? In truth he is the son of the wind. We have never seen another like him."

◈ Sources for this chapter: *Leyenda del Tepozteco* and *Tratado de las idolatriás.*

1. The deer, the sheep, and many other horned animals are common messianic symbols throughout the world's spiritual traditions. In this text, Ce Acatl's hunting of the deer, a solar symbol, prophecies his future messianic role.

CHAPTER TEN
HIS FATHER'S BONES

1 Year Ten Tecpatl (995 C.E.). Ce Acatl was in his ninth year and was developing solid common sense. He asked his grandparents: "Who is my father? Where can I see him?" They answered: "Look son, he was ambushed by some foreigners and is lying over yonder in the sands where he was buried. Others have taken his place and his kingdom."

2 So he said: "I would like to see how my father's face looked!" He then went to the coast and searched and dug until he found the bones. After he unearthed them, he took them to the mountain of Mixcoatl, which is located by the town of Amatlan. In this place he buried them again.[1]

3 His grandparents understood that these actions could bring him harm and were anxious for him. But he reassured them: "Do not fear. I am the lord of transformation. I know what I have to do."

Sources for this chapter: *Anales de Cuautitlán; Leyenda del Tepozteco;* and *Tratado de las idolatrías.*

1. Even now, the remains of a Toltec temple are still there.

CHAPTER ELEVEN

INVITATION TO TULA

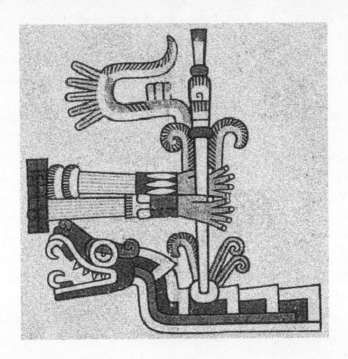

1 Year Thirteen Acatl (959 C.E.). When the princes were notified that Mixcoatl's heir was still alive, they became scared. In common agreement they planned to deceive him in a way that would bring him to the city, and then kill him. So they sent a message to him.

2 "Welcome our son! Why have we not been informed of your existence so that we can rejoice with you and give back to you your inheritance that we have been keeping as a loan? It is not right that we keep it any longer. We want to see you soon.

3 "We have also heard that you found the remains of your father, our brother and lord, and that you gave him an honorable burial. Is that so? We would like to have been of assistance! Here in Tula we have arranged to raise a temple in his memory so that people can offer him sacrifices. Therefore we invite you and your grandfather, the venerable elder, to participate in the funeral rites we have prepared for Mixcoatl."

4 On hearing this invitation a great sorrow overcame Ce Acatl's grandparents. They understood that behind these words there was a plan to annihilate them. But coming near them, Ce Acatl said: "My parents, do not be sad. I will go on my own to see the lords."

5 Cipactonal answered: "No, my son, you are very young and I am an old man. It is appropriate that I should be the one to die. You stay and take care of your grandmother." But the young one insisted: "No, my father, I will go myself; necessity obliges me. I'm on my way. I'm an orphan and I am stalked. I must find my own destiny. Oh, my parents, do not be afraid! Do not fear for what I undertake."

6 Then he asked the messengers: "What is this of my grandfather coming to the ceremony with me? If someone must go then I, the heir, will go alone." To this they answered, "Be it as you wish," after which they departed.

7 Before going, the young one met with the elders and told them: "Tomorrow, very early, before sunrise, look for a cloud in the sky. That will be a signal between us. If it's black, it will mean that I'm dead; if it's white, it will mean that I have won. Believe so." With this agreement they bade him goodbye.

Sources for this chapter: *Anales de Cuautitlán; Leyenda de los soles;* and *Leyenda del Tepozteco.*

CHAPTER TWELVE
THE SACRIFICE

1 When Ce Acatl arrived in Tula, his uncles greeted him: "Be welcome, son! How you have grown! And where is your grandfather, the venerable elder? We want the honor of his greetings." To this Ce Acatl responded: "My grandfather is an old man; his legs do not support him any longer. But here I am, my father's heir. I will fulfill all of his obligations, my uncles!"

2 They told him: "You speak the truth, but what did you bring? What will be your offering to the temple? If you only sacrifice a rabbit, a snake, or butterflies and flowers, the sons of Tlaloc will be angered and perhaps they will want to bring some kind of calamity to your people. This is what you must do: It is necessary that you at least offer a tiger, an eagle, and a wolf. And these three you must find yourself, which is most proper for the ceremony."

3 Their intention was that as he hunted the beasts, they would kill the young one. He answered: "My uncles, what you say is true. For my offering I will do just as you have ordered."

4 After this he went to the mountains and there invoked the spirit of the animals, telling them: "My brothers, come at once! I have been ordered to make an offering of your blood for my father's temple. Do not be afraid, I will seem to tie you by the neck, but this will only be a trick." On hearing this, the animals, with great docility, offered themselves to his leash and came with him to Tula.[1]

5 Seeing him approach, his uncles were astonished and became very angry. Then, making a new plan, they told themselves: "First we will light the sacrificial fire, then we will ask Ce Acatl to go up to the temple with his offerings. When he gets to the top we will kill him; from the top it is easy to fall down the stairs!"

6 But the young one, suspecting such an ambush, called the spirits of the badgers and the moles and told them: "Come, my brothers, drill this temple from the base to the top. Dig the earth and make a tunnel through its structure in such a way that there will be a secret path for me to travel up to the top." And so they did.[2]

7 At sunrise the young one came to the entrance of the secret tunnel. There he called the spirit of the insects and he told them: "Make way, you white and black spiders! Do not be a nuisance! Go your way, night butterflies and lizards! Nothing should stand between me and my uncles, those who exist amidst opulence and live in the higher dwellings."[3]

8 Then he went up through the secret tunnel, appeared in the topmost part of the temple, and shouted: "I am Quetzalcoatl, the son without a father! I have come to look for my uncles, the celestial nobles! Are they not those down there who are ducking like water drops spilling to the ground? I can hardly see you!"

9 Then he added: "Come here, my lords, I am waiting for you! I brought with me my mother's dress and her sword. I will bury it in your throats, in your wombs, in your sides, so you will know that my mother is the one, Chalchiuhtlicue."[4]

10 When they saw him at the top of the temple, his uncles exclaimed, "What is this? We should be the ones to light the fire!" They were very angry and ran up the steps, but the steps were very steep and high and when they arrived at the top, the fire was already burning.

11 Then Ce Acatl called the spirits of the flames and he told them: "Come here, you, my sister, the death! Here you will revive and be reborn. Come to help me, my father, the one of the burning canes, the one of the red hair, you who are father and mother of the gods! Sit on my mat of flowers; come and drink!"[5]

12 The first one to arrive at the temple's summit was Zolton. He fell upon Ce Acatl, but the young one grasped a deep, flat stone vase, hit Zolton on the head, and threw him to the ground. Then Cuilton came, but the fierce animals meant to be sacrificed jumped on Cuilton and tore him to pieces. Then Ce Acatl took both of their bodies and threw them into the fire in which they were totally consumed.

> ✸ Sources for this chapter: *Anales de Cuautitlán* and *Tratado de las idolatrías.*

1. The three animals that were present at the temple were an eagle, an ocelot, and a coyote. The eagle symbolizes the ego, the ocelot is the unconscious or the nocturnal dimension, and the coyote is sexuality. These three are Nahuals, shapeshifters, or animal spirits or alter egos of the being, and each is Ce Acatl's twin.

2. This myth alludes to the ascending of the divine energy. The pyramid is the body; the stairs are the vertebrae; the tunnel underneath is a subtle channel; the animals that drill it are the sleeping forces in the base of the spinal column.

3. The insects represent instinctual fears.

4. "The one of the turquoise skirt"; a deity of the waters and Tlaloc's feminine manifestation.

5. The fire is the vital energy. This myth alludes to the Tlahuizcalpantecuhtli, "the one who makes his home in the light."

CHAPTER THIRTEEN

THE WHITE CLOUD

1 Upon hearing the shouting and screaming of their lords, the guardians ran up to the temple. When they saw the slashed and burned bodies, they became very angry and wanted to arrest the boy. So they searched for him everywhere but did not find him. He had slipped away, sliding down through the tunnel that the badgers and moles had made.

2 As Ce Acatl traveled on his way, the people came out to receive him and applaud him. The reign of the usurpers had been extremely cruel and the imposed tribute on the people had been an overwhelming and heavy burden to carry. So with great joy, the news of the brothers' death spread throughout the land.

3 Upon his arrival at the town of Tepoztlan, the inhabitants came out and welcomed him, saying: "Long live the great man of the sword, the victor over the devourers." They placed him on an *amer*[1] and took him through the streets, and so they recognized him as the son of the king and as the heir of Tula.[2]

4 The next day, early in the morning, his grandparents came out to look at the sky. On seeing that a black cloud was rising over the land, they became very sad and began to cry: "Now our son is lost! He has died!" But after a while the cloud turned as white as the snow and then the elders grew happy: "We have won; our son is the winner!"

 Source for this chapter: *Leyenda del Tepozteco.*

1. "Stretcher."
2. Tepoztecatl, or "the man of the sword," is the name of the dynasty of kings that has reigned in Tepoztlan since that time.

CHAPTER FOURTEEN

THE ENIGMAS OF THE SERPENT

1 Year One Tecpatl (960 C.E.). The young one was fourteen years old when he was sent by his grandparents to the city of Xochicalco to be trained by the priests of Quetzalcoatl. There the priests were raising a very remarkable serpent with seven heads that was named Petlazolcoatl.[1] She would lie across the way of those she would see coming and then ask them questions. If they were not able to respond, she would eat them.

2 She appeared before Ce Acatl and addressed him: "Young one, I have come to tell you that here in this region of the world, the land of our ancestors and the gigantic men and the hunchbacks, and long before the arrival of any of those living today, I was already walking these roads." Then the serpent made seven requests in the language of mystery.

3 This was the first: "Bring me food, my child! Take it to the sun, spread it on my plate, and bury in the middle of its heart the spear of the heavens, and by its side make the great green tiger sit, so he will drink the spilled blood."[2]

4 Ce Acatl answered: "Which other sun if not the Golden Egg, root of the universe? And what spear if not the sacred invocation? And here the precious tiger crouching in front of you is talking with you."

5 Such a response pleased the serpent, and she then offered the second enigma: "Go, child, bring me the brain of heaven, so I can see it! If you are a true man, satisfy my wish. And go carefully."[3]

6 And this is what she was asking for: a load of aromatic incense and a load of perfumes. Then Ce Acatl brought out the offering that he carried with him and burned the incense before the serpent. And she was satisfied.

7 Then again she proposed: "Son, build for me a precious temple with its facade in a straight line and in one piece with the roof. Arrange for a young white female deer dressed with a fine white cape to enter this space, led by the guardian of the white rattle. I will want to hear the rattle! The deer should be stained with the blood of the serpent that comes out of the flower in the center of the rattle. Blood comes out of those that have no mother or father."

8 To this he answered: "What precious temple but the body, and what well-placed roof but the human head? And his vision is the jeweled deer and the rattle that comes with her is his breathing. And who are those that have no mother or father but the orifices of our breathing?"

9 On hearing the response, the serpent came to propose the fourth enigma: "Go back home, son. Go back immediately! If on your return you see fire in the middle of the day, ask your brother to follow you on his knees as a black dog, bringing between his legs the soul of our great mother."

10 So Ce Acatl responded: "Here my house comes with me. The midday fire illuminates it, and my dog that is my shadow and that maintains my purity keeps me company, in which hands I bring my mother's favor."[4]

11 The serpent accepted the answer and offered the fifth enigma: "Run son, search for the heart of heaven and bring it here to me! I want to see it! And with it bring one of the many sons wrapped front and back with a white tunic."

12 He answered: "I did bring it, father. It is here, the heart of heaven is looking at you with me, right from the center of the flower of many buds and the one and only tunic that adorns my head."

13 She then said: "Very well, my son. Now find me the branch of a *ceiba* with three ropes wrapped around it, and it should move like a living reed. This will make my dinner tastier. What do you think, that a stick of ceiba is hard to eat?"[5]

14 Then he answered: "It is hard, my father, but quite delicious. It certainly gives good flavor to food. I carry on my back precisely such a branch, as wavy as a living reed, with three twisted cords around it. I have prepared it for you. Take it."

15 Then the serpent offered her last enigma: "Go now and bring me those round things, like lids that cover the bottom of the well. I want two white ones and two yellow ones. Do you know what I am talking about, my son? If you don't, it will not be possible for you to pass through."

16 He then answered: "I know that, father. Here, the well that you speak of is in my chest. I see in its bottom the yellow and the white seeds you ask for, but if you want to eat them, you should come down to get them."

17 Such mysterious language. When the serpent heard the answers, she became very sad. It had been foretold that the one who understood would be the one to hold power over the people and would come to the king's matting.[6] He would be called a great and true man who would become the new serpent lord. Also great was the suffering of the priests of Xochicalco, for they were punished for their sins of taking children as tribute.

18 Because of his sins, the serpent was overcome. His power ended when the heart of heaven sent the celestial tiger against him, the fearsome Tlaloc Quetzalcoatl,[7] the one who could eat him in his turn. That is how the curse of the enigmas fell upon the serpent: He was outsmarted by the one who answered. And the people of the city, those who had offered their sons for the serpent, saw Ce Acatl and became very happy. For it is said that the people always carry the faults of their lords.

Sources for this chapter: *Cantares de Dzitbalche; Chilam Balam de Chumayel;* and *Chilam Balam de Tuzik.*

1. The serpent is metaphorical, here representing the priestly conclave. Throughout this chapter Ce Acatl is addressing a male priest whose title is Cihuacoatl (lady serpent).
2. This is the essence of the solar myth, the collection of symbolic themes that represent the main characteristics of an avatar.
3. "Brain of heaven" or "heart of heaven" are two names of the divinity. In this context, as in the next, meditation is mentioned as a way of reaching god.
4. This is a game of metaphorical concepts. The dog and the shadow are two images of the tonal or human soul. The midday sun signifies a state of inner illumination. The house signifies Quetzalcoatl's cyclical body, which is frequently represented as a conch shell.
5. The branch, the reed, and other phallic images represent the spinal column, the essential organ in the process of meditation.
6. The "matting" referred to here is akin to a throne.
7. Ce Acatl is Tlaloc's human form, Ometeotl's aspect of fertility.

CHAPTER FIFTEEN
IN THE HOUSE OF PRAYER

1 Year One Calli (973 C.E.). Around that time Ce Acatl was approaching his twenty-seventh birthday. He then departed to the city of Tulantzinco with the intention of being invested according to his lineage. For four years he remained there, in a house of prayer[1] that had in it green stairs. He was in deep meditation when the Toltecs came into his room looking for him.

2 In Tulantzinco he learned everything: how to find the inner divine;[2] how to invoke the one with a skirt of stars that is inside heaven; how to talk to the one with the black dress who makes things manifest;[3] and how to talk to the one with a red suit who gives stability and support to the earth and is movement in the whole of the universe.

3 He also learned to speak from the seat of honor of the dual trinity,[4] the place of the Nine Scales,[5] and with the one who is the substance of heaven and lord of the intimate vicinity.[6] The old ones know that as a supplicant he invoked the dweller, living apart and in meditation.

4 In the fourth year he was invested as a priest of Quetzalcoatl. He was given the reed staff, and around his neck was placed the jewel of the wind. Then the Toltecs came looking for him.

Sources for this chapter: *Códice Chimalpopoca* and *Códice Florentino.*

1. Calmecac, "lined up columns," was the monastery of obligatory education for future kings.
2. Moteotia, "to deify oneself," was a spiritual technique of the ancient Nahuas.
3. Moyocoyani, "the self-created being," is a name of God.
4. Omeyocan, "place of the two-three," is the name of the Nahuas paradise.
5. These people held the belief that there were nine dimensions in the universe.
6. Tloque nahuaque, "owner of that which is near and inseparable," is another name of God.

CHAPTER SIXTEEN
THE KINGDOM

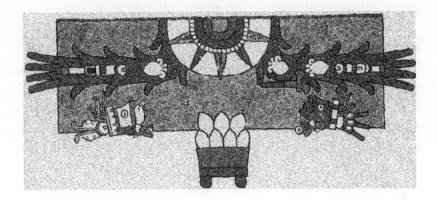

1 Year Five Calli (977 C.E.). The Toltecs came looking for him to ask him to be their king in Tula and also to be their priest. By then he was thirty-one years old. His government was prudent and just. Under his hand the kingdom enjoyed great abundance and its inhabitants were happy, without sorrow or hunger.

2 Ce Acatl schooled the Toltecs and placed by his side clear-thinking men to enhance his kingdom. He employed refined officials who brought beauty to everything they placed their hands on, making everything good, graceful, and useful. Men skilled in many professions were plentiful: mechanics; painters; stoneworkers; carpenters; masons; whitewashers; and artisans of the feather, ceramics, threading, and weaving.

3 He attracted talented people: experts in natural astrology to adjust the accounting of the year;[1] people capable of dream interpretation; wise men who possessed the knowledge of the stars in the heavens to name and calculate the stars' influences and qualities; good and virtuous men; good singers, dancers, rattle and drum players; composers, devoted men, and great orators. In all of them he inspired loyalty.

4 In those times basic food was given away by the kingdom. The corncobs were thick and long, like the hand of a *metate*.² Spoiled corncobs were used to heat up the sweat lodges. The pumpkins were so swollen that a man could hardly hold them. People could climb *bledos* as big as palms. Not a thing was missing in their homes.

5 They also cultivated cotton in a thousand colors: red, yellow, purple, dark blue, brown, all natural and organic. They raised birds with rich and brilliantly colored plumage, precious birds of every lineage, the type that sing beautifully, the kind that warble in the mountains. Cacao was abundant, the most delicious and fine cacao; the cacao plants were raised everywhere, as were beautiful flowers.³

6 Ce Acatl also saw to the development of the arts of mosaic and painting, and the refinement of the art of ceramics. The people ate and drank from plates and glasses glazed with blue, green, and white. They delivered their offerings with fine feathers and decorated their walls with silver. They held as precious shells and stones, while gold was regarded as a thing of little value. Ce Acatl also sought development in the art of bookmaking, and in the profession of mechanics he trained many experts.

7 He ordered altars to be built all over the towns and images to be painted on large walls before which the Toltecs could kneel and kiss the earth in honor of the one for whom we all live. He established that these images and altars should be destroyed every fifty-two years, according to tradition, and replaced with those of even greater splendor.⁴

8 He ordered the carving of the greatest treasure ever to be seen on earth, a game called Tlachtli.⁵ Its size was equal to half of a large room. It was made of innumerable pieces of gold and fine stones the functions of which were very ingenious; four different types of stones—turquoise, garnet, jade, and hyacinth—represented the four ethnicities of the people in his kingdom. There was also a singular stone of carbuncle carved in his image as everyone's king and the first in command. He imparted justice throughout the land with the help of this game.

Sources for this chapter: *Códice Florentino* and *Historia general de las cosas de la Nueva España.*

1. The periodic rectification of the calendar was part of an adjustment that took place every five hundred twenty years. Such adjustments were connected with Quetzalcoatl's and Tezcatlipoca's time periods.
2. A *metate* is a stone for grinding corn.
3. These paradisiacal conditions correspond to the Toltec belief in life after death. At the same time they emphasize the level that Toltec civilization reached in the age of Ce Acatl.
4. The purpose of the cyclical destruction of images and temples was to prevent idolatry.
5. *Tlachtli* is similar to chess.

CHAPTER SEVENTEEN

THE ROYAL HOUSE

1 Ce Acatl said: "Give me a multitude of people, for I need to build my house." At once the Toltecs joined him. He ordered them to bring many stones to a chosen place, as well as everything necessary to build a good house: plenty of lime, shells, precious stones, paint, and gold.

2 When everything was ready, he asked the Toltecs to go home and close their doors. He told them to reinforce their doors and windows as if preparing for a great storm, and that regardless of motives, no one should go out in the streets. They did as they were told.

3 At sunset a great wind came, progressively increasing until it became a storm. The storm rolled throughout the city, scattering the building materials, making terrifying noises, and alarming the Toltecs.[1]

4 By morning the wind had calmed. Then the sound of the trumpet shell was heard, calling the people to gather. They all came out, and there they were, materials and stones properly placed in the shape of a beautiful palace with four chambers oriented toward the four directions.

5 Ce Acatl decorated the interior of the chambers with chosen colors. For the first chamber he chose to cover the walls and floor with ornaments carved in jade; the interior of the second he covered with fine feathers; the third was covered with gold sheets embossed with the most beautiful designs; and the fourth chamber was decorated with pink mother-of-pearl and corals.[2]

6 He also built diverse shadowed places of shadow and penitence in which, in continuous fasting and meditation, he lived apart from everyone. He placed guards at his doors blocking everyone's access. He also made a great temple with columns that were shaped like feathered serpents, but this one was unfinished as an example of humility.[3]

Sources for this chapter: *Leyenda del Tepozteco* and *Anales de Cuautitlán.*

1. This is not an actual historical occurrence, but rather serves to illustrate Ce Acatl as lord of the storms.
2. This house is a reflection of the universe: In the center of its four dimensions consciousness is inserted.
3. For the Toltec, building something too perfect was seen as challenging God. Thus there was always some detail left unfinished in their work.

CHAPTER EIGHTEEN

THE INSIGNIAS

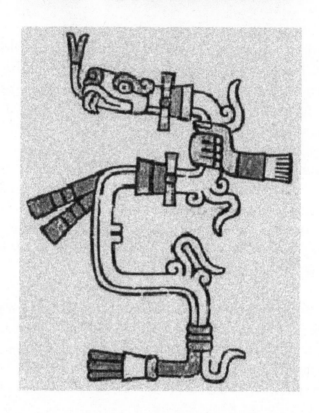

1 Even with all his wealth, Ce Acatl did not forget the one for whom we all live, and lead a virtuous and penitential life. Each night at midnight sharp, he came down to the aqueduct to take a ritual bath and perform his ablutions. There he would offer reparations for all the Toltecs, piercing his ears with needles of precious jade and offering his blood on quetzal feathers for any who had committed sin publicly or in secret. All of his offerings were accompanied by incense from smudging vases.

2 Often he spoke with "the one who lives in the nine heavens," whose name is Wind and Darkness.[1] He said: "Come you, the inhabitant; you, the deity of the four directions, infinite being! Come you, the one from the nine regions, illuminating spirit, force and essence of Tlaloc, Lord Quetzalcoatl!" This is how he invoked his divinity.[2]

3 He also talked to his people. He heard their pleas and imparted justice. All of the inhabitants of the land had access to him and his judgments were just and wise. To impart justice, he wore his penitential dress and the garments and insignias of his station.

4 On his head he set a conical miter made of tiger skin. On his face he wore a beard made from green and yellow feathers. His face, arms, and legs were decorated with black and yellow stripes. He wore spiral-shaped gold earpieces that fell over his shoulder, a shell necklace, and a breastplate, and entwined in his hair were *guacamaya* and quetzal feathers.

5 He wore a short red skirt covering his tights and legs and around his ankles he wore a set of small bells tied with tiger-skin stripes. His sandals were white; his shield was black and red and adorned with the spiral jewel of the wind. His staff was a curved reed of half a measure.

6 This is how he would be seen by everyone. Later, in his private sleeping quarters, he would put on his black gown and loosen his hair.

> ❀ Sources for this chapter: *Anales de Cuautitlán; Tratado de las idolatrías;* and *Códice Florentino*.

1. Yohualli Ehecatl, "wind and darkness," implying invisible and intangible.
2. In this way he attempted to reach or earn a divine condition.

PART TWO

I drank wine from mushrooms,
And my heart is tormented.

CHAPTER ONE
TEZCATLIPOCA

1 It happened that Ce Acatl's heart was careless, and in the midst of opulence the Toltec people became negligent. Certain obscure hearts were jealous of the kingdom and incited people to do wrong, to be adulterous, and to offend the heavens with profane ceremonies.[1]

2 As a consequence of their neglect, the Toltecs began to fall and suffer calamities. The one for whom we all live also forgot them. Therefore, many of them thought about migrating to new regions, and many turned their backs on the cult of Quetzalcoatl.

3 Seeing this, the enemies of Tula made an alliance against the city and came with a great army. Even the "wild people" who lived on the frontiers came into the land and established themselves in various places, committing iniquity and introducing a new cult that no one had known before.[2]

4 The initiator of all this decadence was Tezcatlipoca, a very brave and clever sorcerer who was lord over great regions of the earth.[3] In his perversity he was assisted by his helpers, the ones named Yaotl[4] and Ce Tecpatl.[5] The three of them dwelled in a refuge under the earth.

5 Tezcatlipoca was the one who introduced into the kingdom the sacrifice of men. Many times the sorcerers tried to persuade the king to allow human sacrifices and the killing of men, but he never wanted such sacrifices and never allowed them, for he loved his people. This attitude made the evil ones angry, so they resolved to punish the king and make him leave the city.[6]

6 With sweet and reasonable words, Tezcatlipoca was luring the Toltecs. He exercised his powers. He numbed them with his breath and easily persuaded them to commit abominable and ugly acts. Everywhere he went he exhorted, threatened, and intimidated the people into giving up their good habits. To reach his goals he took on different personalities: He transformed his body into animal shapes and monstrous beings, and he made himself appear as a female prostitute. He also shaved his head, which had been neither seen nor done before.

7 The elders tell that this god came from heaven, sliding down on a rope woven of spider thread,[7] and that he came to the world with the mission of destroying Quetzalcoatl's people so that he himself would become king and deity.

⊛ Source for this chapter: *Historia general de las cosas de la Nueva España.*

1. The cruel Tezcatlipoca cults appeared in Mesoamerica each time a civilization began to decline. Their main characteristic was the imposition of human sacrifices.
2. The "wild people" (or Chichimecas) were groups of northern tribes who moved south, looking for better living conditions. The Aztecs were one such group.
3. Tezcatlipoca, also called "Smoking Mirror," is the symbol of relativity or cosmic illusion and embodies the renovating power of nature. It is the supreme divinity of the Nahuatl pantheon. In this story it is presented as an impersonal male deity who speaks through his priests.
4. Yaotl means "enemy" or "war."
5. Meaning "one stone," Ce Tecpatl is Mixcoatl's calendar name and is also the name of the father of Quetzalcoatl, who returns as an avenger.
6. This episode refers to the time in which the peace-loving cult of the feathered serpent was substituted for the heroic model of Tezcatlipoca and Huitzilopochtli.
7. For Indo-americans the spider was the symbol of the impersonal deity, weaver of the strings of destiny.

CHAPTER TWO
THE LOAD OF FIREWOOD

1 The ancients foretold many signals of Tezcatlipoca's coming. The signs began like this: Tezcatlipoca sent a message to Ce Acatl to warn him of his presence. There was a Toltec wood gatherer on the mountain going about his work. He had collected a great load of wood and was about to return home when before him there appeared a very old man who spoke these words:

2 "Toltec! By any chance do you happen to know Ce Acatl, the penitent?" To this the wood gatherer answered: "Yes, my lord, he is our beloved sovereign."

3 Once again the old man spoke: "Toltec! It is important that you run to the palace where Ce Acatl is in hiding. Tell him that an old priest has arrived and he is asking for Ce Acatl to meet with him alone on top of Xicoco mountain.[1] There he will receive a most important message."

4 But the Toltec answered: "My father, this cannot happen because he is fasting in hiding and his palace is very well protected by numerous guardians. He is only to be bothered for urgent matters."

5 Then the old man answered: "Do not fear. He will listen to you. If he asks for the priest's identity, you must tell him this: *He declares that he is representing the king, your father, and he dwells on the other side of the world.* On hearing this they will allow you to enter the palace."

6 But the Toltec did not want to go, so he insisted: "I cannot respect your wishes, grandfather, until you give me a precise signal of your identity."

7 Then pointing to the wood the old man asked: "What is that?" To this the wood gatherer answered: "It is only dead wood that your servant is collecting here and there." Then the old man reached out with his open hand over the pile of wood, which immediately was covered with green shoots and many flowers, and he said to the Toltec: "Take a branch to the penitent and he will listen to you."

8 So, full of fear, the wood gatherer went away to tell the king that a magician had appeared to him at the top of the mountain and asked to speak to him alone about a very important matter. But Ce Acatl answered him: "I cannot go alone to meet him. By law I have to consult with my ministers." And so he did.

9 The ministers' advice was that Ce Acatl should go to verify the prodigy, but that he should be accompanied by a small body of guards and a few interpreters of divine matters. "It might happen that there would be an ambush and you might be killed or bewitched," they told him.

10 Up the Xicoco they went and there they saw the old man. Ce Acatl stepped forward and while giving his greetings told him: "Venerated grandfather, is it you that is looking for me? Perhaps you are bringing me a message from my father?"

11 But the old man answered: "Do not make fun of me, my lord. I am only a poor old wandering man. I have no home and am just passing by, looking for some crumbs to eat. I do not know in any way what you are talking about." On hearing this answer Ce Acatl returned to the city, annoyed and worried, asking himself what kind of warning this could be. This was the first of the many foretold signs.

Source for this chapter: *Leyenda del Tepozteco*.

---

1. Xicoco (beehive) is an esoteric name for the conclave of initiates and is also the name of the mountain that dominates Tula's landscape. According to the tradition that is preserved even today, the mountain is hollow and there the workers of darkness hold their sessions.

CHAPTER THREE

THE WHORES

1 On a certain night, according to his custom, the king came down to the aqueduct to take his bath. There he encountered two women who were waiting for him. When he saw them he asked, "Who are you?" To this they answered: "We are your servants, travelers from the country of Zapotlan. Because of some aggravations we have come to you in demand of counsel and justice."

2 So he answered: "Very well ladies, but we cannot meet here. We must meet in my dwellings, but for that it is necessary that you ask for an audience." And as they were very persistent, he gave orders to his guards to let them in.[1]

3 The next day these women, dressed as whores, came to the doors of the royal house, where they were admitted. This was seen by the whole town, and the Toltecs began to talk about it.

4 Ce Acatl did not know that these women were Tezcatlipoca and his helpers who had transformed themselves in this way. Their objective was to punish the king by corrupting the people of Tula through their example.

5 In fact, when others saw that the whores were frequenting the palace, some of the women of higher status also started going to the sanctuaries and temples, though not in processions or for offerings. They would go instead to engage in sinful excesses with the priests, desecrating the penitential rooms and performing serious and abominable crimes.

6 One of these participants was a lady of the royal house, a very noble princess close to the king. During a visit in celebration of the anniversary of the great temple in the city of Cholula, she took part in such acts with terrible consequences.

7 Among the attending monks there was one called Huiztli. He saw the woman and was solicited by her and incited to transgression, and he offered his friendship. As a consequence of their sin, after a time she gave birth to a boy whom she named Colotl,[2] and from the time of his birth Colotl was hidden in the temple.

8 In the face of these events Ce Acatl did not know what to do, and so he remained secluded within his chambers, practicing his meditations and living in austerity. He would only leave his rooms to go to the aqueduct or to the ball-game fields where he would pray.[3]

🔲 Sources for this chapter: *Anales de Cuautitlán; Historia general de las cosas de la Nueva España;* and *Relaciones históricas.*

---

1. An encounter by a water fountain with a whore is a typical occurrence in the solar myth.
2. "Scorpion,"
3. This field, in the shape of an *H,* was used as a place for ceremonial offerings and prayers. The ball game itself held ritual meaning in Mesoamerica

CHAPTER FOUR
THE SONS OF TLALOC

1 One day the king went to his shrine in the field of the ballgame. Tezcatlipoca sent the sons of Tlaloc against him. In this way and without knowing it, he played against Tlaloc's sons.

2 They asked him: "Oh prince, what will you give us if we win the game?" He answered: "If you defeat me I will give you my precious stones and my quetzal crowns." Then they assured him, "That is precisely what we will give you if you win; our precious stones and our green feathers."

3 Ce Acatl won the game. When he demanded his prize, the sons of Tlaloc brought the accorded objects, but instead of turquoises they gave him grains of corn and instead of feathers they gave him the green leaves of the maize. They told him: "Here is your prize; these are our jewels."

4 But he did not want to take them. "Is this what I have won? These are not precious stones and fine feathers. I will not accept these, you liars!" Then the sons of Tlaloc took their grain and corn leaves, saying: "Very well, if that is what you wish, we will hide our jewels and our feathers." And they threw them into a nearby water stream.

5 Then, turning to the king, they told him: "You will bring hardship to the Toltecs. Now you will know hunger. You will go from the well to the caverns and will walk the streets asking for crumbs. Your voices will travel in the night, asking for a sip of water. Where to drink water? Where to eat at least some leftover corn?"

6 "Sunken will be the heart of the Toltecs over their banquet of stones and firewood. The rigor of hunger will be your bread for four years. Years of violent fighting, years of fire in the world, this we promise you, oh prince. Fear will be your food all over the kingdom." After speaking so, they threw themselves into the water and disappeared. Ce Acatl was left somber and confused.

Sources for this chapter: *Anales de Cuautitlán* and *Chilam Balam, libro de los libros.*

CHAPTER FIVE

THE HUNGER

1 After this a drought occurred. For four years the land was without water. First, ice fell and covered the ground knee-deep, which ruined seeds and fruits. Then the sun burned and dried up all the trees, cactuses, and agaves. Stones blew up into pieces from the heat. The Toltecs experienced very hard times, the beginning of their punishment for their sins accumulating before the heavens. And the clamor of the people lifted up all the way to the royal house.

2 On a certain day a messenger came before the king: "Oh brother, our prince, Ometeotl's wrath is falling on us. His lightning is consuming us. Stones, darts, arrows: That is what the one for whom we all live has sent to the miserable of this world.

3 "I come to tell you of the needs of the humble ones among your people. They spend the night with nothing to eat, and nothing they have when dawn comes again. See for yourself! Your little brothers are suffering great poverty. They cross mountains and valleys to find hardly enough sustenance for one day.

4 "They move about in fear, their faces and bodies like images of death. They sit sadly against the walls and on the corners, biting their nails and looking at the mouths of those passing by, waiting for a good word. Their sons go naked with their faces yellow like the color of earth, and in the night they all tremble with cold. They are crying and all of their bones can be counted. Oh pain!" So the messenger spoke.

5 On hearing such news Ce Acatl fell down, overwhelmed with sorrow, for within himself he understood that what had offended Ometeotl was his fault and was due to his own negligence.

🕸 Sources for this chapter: *Anales de Cuautitlán; Historia general de las cosas de la Nueva España;* and *Códice Florentino.*

CHAPTER SIX

PETITION TO TLALOC

1 The next day, while it was still dark, he came out of his house and walked toward Tlaloc's temple. On his face could be seen the signs of insomnia and torment. On arriving at the temple he asked the guardian-minister: "Make the sanctuary ready and pray with me, for the people have urgent need of Ometeotl."

2 Then everything was prepared in the sanctuary. The image of the altar was smudged and prostrating himself before it, Ce Acatl prayed: "Oh Lord, you our generous and magnanimous deity of the plants and humid places. Lord of the water's paradise! You, the aromatic and flowery spirit of incense!

3 "See our pain, see humble people who are suffering, lost in hunger. See our ears that look like those of the dead, our dry mouths like *esparto*.[1] Look how the four-legged creatures in dismay suck and lick the earth, look at the birds and take pity on them. It greatly grieves one to see them with their fallen wings and their mouths open from thirst. See how the people faint and die.

4 "God of sustenance, giver of life, what is this? Are you using your curved fangs on the weak, on those as thin as a green reed? How determined is your heart? Is it foretold that the Toltec will perish and that the place where he lives will become wild and a desert of rocks? Will the temples fall? Will your darts of wrath be spent on us?

5 "Oh Deity! Is it possible that this wrath is not for the correction but for the total destruction of your people? For your punishment is prevailing on us. Let it be like the one from the father and mother who are educating their children. You well know that the people are like children, holding no grudges because of repression.

6 "Now restrain death, the messenger that is hungry and thirsty for us, the dwellers of this place. And if my sin has been such that I deserve no redemption, give me at least this: that the innocent, the ones who do not know how to walk and who play with stones, be provided with bread.

7 "Take pity on the poor, the ones who have never known what a good day is. Forgive your warriors, who in a moment would give their lives for your name. If my offenses, Lord, have gone up to the heavens and come down to hell, and the stench from my faults extends unto the confines of the world, let me be destroyed. But do take it on yourself to console those who are living on the face of the earth.

8 "Scatter your smoke and quench your fire. Come, clear serenity. Birds, come to bask and sing in the sun. Give the birds peace so that they get to know you and take me for all my sins."

9 After speaking in this manner, Ce Acatl took a cup of water and spilled it around the fire and toward the four directions saying: "Oh you sons of Tlaloc, spirits of the waters that are holding the four corners of the world and dwell in underground caves and between high mountains! To you who have the power over fountains and tempests, from my heart I call! Come to water the earth! See that the eyes of those who live here are depending on you. I plead . . . come!"

 Source for this chapter: *Códice Florentino.*

1. "Dry grass."

CHAPTER SEVEN

THE BLOOD DEMANDS

1 On a certain day a son of Tlaloc appeared in a fountain that sprang up by Chapultepec. A Toltec baron was there, seated by the water. On seeing a plate full of milled and tender corn coming from the bottom of the fountain, the baron bent over the water and ate it.

2 From within the water a green priest appeared. Looking out and referring to the corn, he said, "Toltec! Do you know what this is?" And the Toltec answered: "Yes, my lord, but here we lost it long ago."

3 Again the tlaloque[1] spoke: "Very well, sit and eat. Meanwhile I will go and talk with my lord." On saying this he went back into the water and disappeared from sight. But he did not take too long in coming back, and when he did he was carrying an armload of excellent young corn.

4 He then said to the baron: "Toltec, take this and bring it to Ce Acatl, the lord of Tula. And when you are delivering it to him you must say this: *Prince! Heaven has taken upon itself suspension of the punishment that was inflicted on your people because of you. But in exchange it asks for the flesh of the daughter of the king of the Mexicans.[2] While heaven is eating her, sustenance will come to you and your people and you will eat, too.*"

5 Immediately the Toltec went to the king's palace and transmitted Tlaloc's orders. On hearing such an order Ce Acatl was overcome with fear and said bitterly: "So be it! Only death can give us life. But will we not end up finishing each other?" He was very confused, for he understood that the demand for blood was a signal of the end of his people. Then turning to the messenger he asked him to tell no one of the matter.

> ✸ Sources for this chapter: *Anales de Cuautitlán* and *Cantares de los Mexicanos.*

1. This refers to the son of Tlaloc as well as to the *tlaloque* (spirit) of the fountain, one of the four hundred deities of vegetation.
2. "Mexicans" in the text are Aztecs.

CHAPTER EIGHT

THE DAUGHTER OF THE MEXICANS

1 But the news was not hidden for very long. Tezcatlipoca knew the urgent demands of Tlaloc's sons and went everywhere voicing them, seducing the people with promises of bread. The Toltecs were famished, thirsty, and willing to do anything to placate the heavens.

2 So Tezcatlipoca sent two of his helpers to the mountain of Xicoco, where the Mexicans were living at that time. He ordered them to ask for the king's daughter, a young maiden named Quetzalli, who was barely more than a child.

3 On arriving at Xicoco the messengers said: "We have come on the orders of Ce Acatl, king of Tula who says that the sons of Tlaloc have appeared and are asking for a Mexican maiden in exchange for food. You, Toxcuecuex, chieftain of the Aztecs, must give us your daughter."

4 With such news the Mexicans became very sad, but as they were a very scattered and weak people, they were not able to oppose the royal orders. They fasted for four days, mourning the death of the maiden. After that time the messengers took her, and her father accompanied her to Tula.

5 On arriving in Tula, Tezcatlipoca ordered the Toltecs: "Quickly take her and sacrifice her over there!" They did as they were told and in that way was a young maiden offered for the sins of the people. This was the beginning of the sacrifice of human beings in ceremonial offerings.

Source for this chapter: *Anales de Cuautitlán.*

CHAPTER NINE

THE CHOICE OF THE MEXICANS

1 The chieftain of the Mexicans was very sad and his heart was bitter. But the sons of Tlaloc came to him and said: "Toxcuecuex! Why are you so heartbroken? Come alone with us to the place where your daughter has been sacrificed, and bring with you a cup."

2 Then the sons of Tlaloc went with Toxcuecuex to the temple to look among the offerings, and there they found the maiden's heart. They took it and placed it in the chieftain's cup along with some grains of corn and incense. When they gave the cup to Toxcuecuex they told him:

3 "Here, from now on this is the food that Mexicans will eat, corn and human blood. A new law and a new government are near, for the time of the Toltecs has come to an end. Go to your people and prepare them."[1]

4 Then the chieftain of the Aztecs went back to his people and told them all that had happened. Knowing that their time was coming, he moved his camp to the border of the kingdom.

> Source for this chapter: *Anales de Cuautitlán.*

1. The maiden symbolizes the virgin earth that is immolated in the process of cultivating the corn. This story contains a psychological justification for the Aztec interpretation of the teachings of Quetzalcoatl: The human sacrifices are seen as a punishment for the sins committed by the Toltecs, and at the same time as payment for the unjust sacrifice of the maiden.

CHAPTER TEN

THE HUMAN SACRIFICES

1 The next day the earth was covered by a cloud, after which it rained. Day and night the earth drank water, for it was dry and thirsty. Then different fruits sprouted up and all the plants became green. Then the Toltecs planted in the earth, and after twenty and forty days the corncobs were swollen.[1] Soon after in that year the human offerings were made.

2 The inhabitants of Tula were very happy. Many of them, grateful to Tezcatlipoca, began to follow his accomplices and participate in the terrifying ceremonies, just as he ordered, saying: "Only in this way, by opening humans and removing their skin, will the gods remain calm."

3 The cult spread everywhere, for the people were persuaded that through human offerings the time of hunger would be conjured away. In fact, many of the Toltecs would voluntarily offer themselves to be immolated.

4 It is told that the practice of human sacrifice was first performed in the place named the Despeñadero. In this place there was a woman from the Otomi nation who was preparing agave leaves in the river. Tezcatlipoca took her, sacrificed her, skinned her, and placed her skin on Xiuhmazatl, one of his followers, who in this way became the first priest of Xipe Toltec.[2]

5 After this a poor warrior, who was dragging his pain all over the city, spent the last of his assets on a banquet of bread and birds for his friends. He then went to the fountain in Chapultepec where an old lady sat selling paper flags and exhorting everyone to go to offer themselves for sacrifice. The little old lady was Tezcatlipoca himself, who in this way was seducing everyone with promises of eternity.

6 So the warrior bought a flag and with the old lady presented himself before the priests. They killed him then by cutting off his head and afterward stuck it on a pole and placed the pole on a platform. This is how the cult of the heads began.[3]

7 There was a group of specially trained women who called themselves the Mothers of Filth.[4] They first appeared in the land of the Cuextecas, where they captured several men. Then quickly they came by pilgrimage to the city of Tula, bringing with them their captives, who were serving them as husbands.

8 As they entered the city, they told their captives: "We are already in Tula. We will have a celebration. Up until now there have never been human sacrifices performed by piercing with arrows. We will initiate that tradition; we will put arrows into your bodies." When the captives heard this, they broke down crying.

9 Once in the city the women celebrated a feast in honor of Tlazolteotl.[5] This feast was called House of Stones. They took two of the captives, painted their bodies in blue, adorned them with fine jewels, and then tied them to a pole. Then they sang a song and danced around them. The song went like this:

10 "Pierce him, pierce him, and throw an arrow again! All this without stopping the dancing, for that is what is proper for the good warriors, the chosen ones to serve the beautiful Lord. Just as the sun appears through the woods in the east, so appears the warrior with his arrows. The warrior gives all of himself." While the women sang, they threw arrows at their captives until they bled to death. It was the first time the people had seen such a ceremony in this land.

11 All of these were the foretold signs that Hueman the astrologer sent as news of the end of the Toltecs. And the king, not knowing how to proceed, dedicated himself with renewed effort to austerity.

⬡ Sources for this chapter: *Historia general de las cosas de la Nueva España; Códice Chimalpopoca;* and *Cantares de Dzitbalche.*

1. "Twenty and forty" here refers to two different stages of the cycle of corn.
2. "Our skinned lord." He represents the corncob and the ascension of the human soul.
3. Also known as the Tzompantli cult, or "the graveyard of the heads," which reached its climax in the times of the Mexicans.
4. A cult order of women adept to Tlazolteotl, Mother Earth, devourer of impurities.
5. This refers to Tlazolteotl the garbage eater. It is another name for Mother Earth.

CHAPTER ELEVEN

THE OLD WOMAN

1 Another sign occurred. In a temple in Tula there was a great statue, which had at its core a black stone. Such a stone was very much appreciated by the Toltecs, because through it, it was possible to talk with Ometeotl. Several guards kept watch over the stone.

2 One day, Tezcatlipoca came to the temple and, resorting to his magical arts, he blew his breath over the guards, putting them to sleep. Then he went to the oracle room, found the statue, and overturned it, breaking it into pieces. Then he put the black stone in his shoulder bag and took it with him to the underground dwellings where he lived.

3 When they woke up, the guards looked everywhere for the stone. While they were busy searching, an old woman came to the temple and said to them: "My sons, I know where to find what you are looking for. My lord Tezcatlipoca has it. He has sent me to show you the place. Don't you see it? It is kept in the depths underneath this room."

4 The old woman teased them with such words and before they could capture her, she disappeared. The king was told of all this, but he said nothing.

✸ Sources for this chapter: *Historia general de las cosas de la Nueva España* and *Teogonía historia e Mexicanos.*

CHAPTER TWELVE
THE WHITE CHILD

1 And another sign occurred. In the west of the city there was a mountain at whose summit a white child appeared, very blond and beautiful and very tall. He remained seated on a rock. The inhabitants of the region were in great awe, asking each other: "Brother, who is this?"[1]

2 Then they stalked him until they were able to capture him. They took him to Tula to present him to the king, but when they were in the middle of the city he began to change. His beauty transformed and he opened his toothless and strange mouth and from it a substance with a filthy, penetrating odor began to pour.

3 When Ce Acatl saw the transformed boy he ordered his guards: "Take that apparition to the place where you found him!" For he saw this as a bad omen. But when they tried to move him, the strange child started to rebel with the force of a god. He threw his captors and grew even taller.

4 Then the guards killed him, opened his body, and observed that he had nothing inside: no heart, no guts, no blood. His head began to rot right away. A terrible stench started to come from the creature and spread throughout the city, contaminating the Toltecs.

5 When the guards saw this, they wrapped the creature in a net and tried to drag him, but it was not possible. The being broke the net's strings, lifted himself from the ground, and, after dying, started to walk across the city, breaking and dragging everything along his path.

6 In the air a voice screamed: "We must bury this dead one! Let's take him far, for his stench will provoke death! Let's drag him!"

7 So the Toltecs found some new ropes and they tried to capture the being, but it was not possible, for the weight and size of the child kept increasing. It had been easy to bring him into the city, but to take him out was not possible.

8 Again the speaker in the sky spoke: "Come, brothers, all of you, let us all come to take this being. Bring your nets to throw death far away!"

9 Then all the citizens gathered, young and old, screaming and yelling, motivating each other to capture the child. They tied him up with eight thick ropes, pulling with great force,[2] but the ropes broke and those who were pulling rolled on the ground, crashing into each other. In the midst of all this confusion some of the people died, for there were many trying to carry the child.

10 Then again up in the air the voice was heard advising the Toltecs in this way: "Brothers! In order to uproot death it is necessary that we sing his song." And so Tezcatlipoca, who was among the multitude giving voice, led the chant, which went like this: "Tie him up, move him, and throw him into the sea. Let him be thrown out, the filth eater!"

11 Finally the chanting put the child to sleep. Then, with the intention of throwing him into the water, they dragged him toward a lake near a mountain of rocks. Many people congregated to see the great child pass by.

12 But once they grew close to the water, the child awoke again, showing the strength of gods. He jumped up from the ground, taking off from the earth.[3] He dragged with him to great heights many of the men that were entangled with the ropes.

13 A large number of those who breathed in the stench that came from the water fell ill and died. The epidemic spread, for the odor overwhelmed all with its filth. Death passed wherever the wind took her, and the land was left in great desolation.

> ✺ Sources for this chapter: *Códice Chimalpopoca* and *Relaciones históricas.*

1. The white child is the symbol of telluric forces. This episode reveals that such forces were unleashed as a consequence of abusing esoteric knowledge. Hallucinogenic mushrooms and the hallucinogenic plants peyote, morning glory, and jimson weed represent this knowledge.
2. The eight ropes, or Chicuei Malinalli, is the symbolic name for the hallucinogenic plants. This whole episode is an allegory of the Toltecs' alienation.
3. The being was a Tlaloque, whose vital element is water.

CHAPTER THIRTEEN

THE NECROMANCER

1 Not yet satisfied with the damage that he provoked, the sorcerer Tezcatlipoca worked out another scheme to deceive the people of Tula. Taking advantage of the market hours, he came to the center of the plaza where everyone could see him. Then on his left hand he conjured a little artificial dancing man.

2 On seeing this, buyers and merchants surrounded the magician to admire him. But while trying to get a closer look, the confusion was such that they stepped on each other, hurting themselves. The magician continued playing with his little man.

3 At a given moment a voice was carried by the wind, enticing the people: "What is the meaning of this, brothers? It is sorcery that is

making the little man dance! Look at this magician, he is a necro-
mancer! Let's kill him with stones! Immediately!"

4 And so they did. They joined together in an uprising and with
stones they killed the magician. There where he fell with his little
man, they smashed him with stones. In the heat of the action, the
Toltecs did not know their mistake.

5 Then the voice spoke again, screaming: "What have you done,
you sinners? Why have you wronged that venerated old man? The
darts of the demon have made you all insane!"

6 At that moment the people heard the flapping of the wings of a
bird in the sky and a great white heron passed over the plaza. She
was flying far from the earth but was visible for the merchants who
were looking at her in great awe: She was pierced by a spear. At the
same time, far on the horizon, they saw the great chain of the
Zacatepec mountains burning. The fire started on its own with great
flames.

7 As all of this occurred, the Toltecs screamed to each other: "Oh
brothers! Our fortune is over, we are dying! The world of culture is
disappearing and barbarism is back! What will become of us, unfortunate ones? Where can we go to be saved?"

> ✸ Source for this chapter: *Historia general de las cosas de la
> Nueva España*.

CHAPTER FOURTEEN

FLOODS AND PLAGUES

1 A few days later an enormous rock fell on Tula, and many smaller stones rained on the inhabitants. This they took as divine retribution. While these were falling, a great storm unleashed itself and then a time of great and violent rains began destroying many of the city's great edifices. The rain went on for almost one hundred days without stopping. The Toltecs thought that these were their final days.

2 They prayed to Tlaloc, asking him in his great mercy to placate the waters. And then the skies cleared. But after the rain ceased falling, a great plague of locusts fell on the earth and devoured every green plant.

3 After the locusts there came worms. Insects were everywhere, eating everything. All the barns and silos were destroyed. The food that was not contaminated by the insects became sour, fermenting so that it could not be eaten. Because of hunger, the people panicked.

4 The people had been greatly deceived by the heavens and many of them were killed. During all of this Ce Acatl meditated on the prophecies and suffered great torment in a corner of his house.

> ✦ Sources for this chapter: *Historia general de las cosas de la Nueva España* and *Anales de Cuautitlán.*

CHAPTER FIFTEEN

THE MIGRATIONS

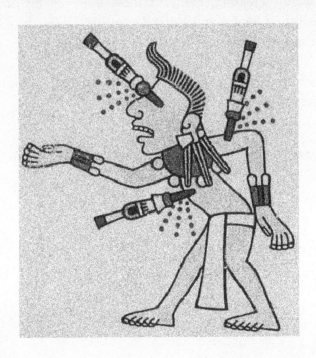

1 In the midst of all these calamities, the voice of a venerated priest was heard throughout the kingdom as he walked throughout the land with his crosier, exhorting in this way: "Brothers, these are the gods' signals that they are angry with us because we have not given them enough food. The kingdom is damned, corrupted is the earth! Where can we go on this terrible day?"

2 With these words he attracted the multitudes, and then he advised them: "Let us abandon our crops, seal our houses, and save our lives. For if we remain tied to our city and our property, time will only bring wrongs, ruin, and calamity upon us. It is not possible to escape from the wrath of time or to change the words of the prophecies."

3 And so he went on convincing the Toltecs to follow him, offering himself as a guide to take them to safety in lands of quiet and rest. Seeing the afflicted inhabitants all around them and how the catastrophes were increasing, many of them followed his advice and abandoned their houses and crops. Groups of Toltecs traveled from their lands, some to the north and others to the east.

4 This venerated priest was none other than Tezcatlipoca, scheming to uproot Ce Acatl from his kingdom.

⚏ Source for this chapter: *Historia general de las cosas de la Nueva España.*

CHAPTER SIXTEEN

THE DANCE IN THE GARDEN

1 Seeing, however, that his plans were not reaching their conclusion, the sorcerer came to design a final scheme for the Toltecs. In the outskirts of Tula, the king had some gardens named Xochicalco.[1] The chief gardener there was a man named Tequihua.[2]

2 The gardener was ambushed by Tezcatlipoca and killed, and his body was hidden among the reeds. Then, taking on Tequihua's appearance, Tezcatlipoca sent a herald into Tula with instructions to command all the inhabitants of the city to come to the gardens:

3 "Citizens! Get moving! You are expected by the gardeners in the region of the Tequihua gardens to do maintenance work. After finishing the labor, we will dance to the rhythm of the drums."

4 Promptly many Toltecs gathered their wives and children and went with all their tools to the gardens of the king. Everyone attended. When the work was done, the gardeners gave wine to all who had come and played the drums, and all the people began to dance.

5 It was a demonic dance. The men jumped up, spinning, and raising their arms and hands. The beat of the drumss grew louder. The dancers were undulating, lifting themselves in waves that broke like a spell on the people. They all followed the voice of the chief gardener.

6 It was a new chant, never heard before in the kingdom. Its words were long, in a language that nobody comprehended. Everyone repeated the phrases that Tequihua was singing, for he had asked that everyone follow the chant with precise accuracy.

7 The dance began at the setting of the sun, and by midnight the trumpets blasted. Then the movement grew more frantic and the rhythm of the spinning became more heated. The Toltecs were bewitched, not realizing that step by step they were being led to a precipice below which there opened a great abyss. Once on the edge, they would jump without knowing what they were doing or looking where they were going. As the gardener was singing his chant, they crowded together and pushed each other toward the empty space.

8 Over the abyss there was a stone bridge where many dancers had gathered. In that moment Tezcatlipoca released a great scream, breaking the foundations of the bridge so that all the dancers tumbled down and were buried under the falling stones.

9 Some of the people tried to escape by climbing up the walls of the ravine. With a sledgehammer, Tezcatlipoca broke the heads of those who managed to reach the top. Many men, too many to count, died by his hand.

10 As a finishing blow, he destroyed the dams that protected the cultivated land. The water flowed into the gardens with great violence and the Toltecs perished, drowned with their working tools.

Sources for this chapter: *Historia general de las cosas de la Nueva España* and *Códice Chimalpopoca.*

1. This means "place of flowers" and is not to be confused with the town south of Tenochtitlan.
2. This means "the builder" and is the title of the Toltecs as initiated people. This episode symbolizes the replacement of a literary cult with esoteric knowledge.

CHAPTER SEVENTEEN

THE DEFORMED DEER

1 Ce Acatl was informed of these calamities: how strangers were appearing in the city, imposing terrible traditions upon the inhabitants of Tula. He also knew that many Toltecs were fleeing the city. Realizing that his continuous practice of penitence in the darkness of the night was useless, Ce Acatl asked his ministers for advice.

2 They told him that in order to placate the wrath from heaven, it was necessary to gather all the people—men, women, children, the elderly, priests, lords, and warriors—for they all had sinned. They should all show, with their offerings and their tears, that they had repented for all of their transgressions.

3 A proclaimer was sent to every place within the kingdom, calling lords and vassals to the city of Tula to participate in a collective offering. On the chosen day a great multitude gathered. According to his means, each one brought something as an offering for the fire.

4 By the afternoon the drums sounded, the army lined up with their flags, and the priests prepared the smudging cups. Ce Acatl, wearing his priestly insignias, went to the top of Mixcoatl's temple and pleaded from deep within his heart:

5 "Oh, our brave and humane Lord, under whose wings we find shelter! You that are fog and wind, you that are peace! I come to tell you with pain that we, here in the city, are living in darkness, without motives or feelings. The people don't greet each other, no one takes others into account, because everyone has lost all hope of receiving help, and all are living in obfuscation, like drunks.

6 "Examples of your wrath have fallen upon us and we are entangled with the forces of evil under whose assault we are ready to sin. We wish that our tribulations came from war, from the heat of the sun! For then the brave would feel great pleasure and would dance.

7 "Ometeotl, it is within your power to give peace and sweetness, richness and prosperity, for you alone are the master of goodness. I plead then, that you take pity on your sheep. I plead for a piece of your tenderness and say that in truth we have a great need of it.

8 "I plead for some days of rest for our people, like those who relish for a few hours the ephemeral beauty of flowers that dry and, as your heart orders, become deities. We are relying on your answer. You are our shelter, prince of darkness, our peace and quiet."

9 Just before he finished his prayer a deformed deer came into the plaza dragging his tail. A roaring of fear passed through the multitude as they watched. The deer went directly to the king and there, in front of everyone, it disappeared. This vision was taken as a negative answer from heaven.

Sources for this chapter: *Historia general de las cosas de la Nueva España* and *Códice Florentino*.

CHAPTER EIGHTEEN

THE CONSPIRACY

1 When the highest ministers saw these signals they started to mistrust the king. Their conclusion was that the king was responsible for the progressive destruction of the people. Accordingly, they gathered in conspiracy to scheme his impeachment and ousting from Tula.

2 The faction of those who were unhappy grew larger, and among them were those on the Council of Tezcatlipoca. On a certain day the priests and lords gathered and said to themselves: "That is enough! Oh lords, the government is perishing. It is necessary that the king leave the throne and that we firmly take over." And they asked each other: "But how will we do this, oh lords?"

3 Disguised by priestly robes, Tezcatlipoca, who was among the conspirators, spoke up: "The king is strong in his penitential disciplines. We will do it like this: Let us make wine and give it to him so that he will lose the strength that supports him, and in this way he will give up his austerity. Then we will be able to expel him."

4 All the ministers accepted this, but the perverse Tezcatlipoca continued: "Before we do this, it is necessary that we go to his retreat and make him know his body."[1]

5 How can we repeat the consultations of the ministers? Their hearts were heavy with their decisions and Quetzalcoatl's ordeal, and without knowing it they were shaping the final ruin of the Toltecs.

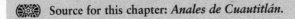 Source for this chapter: *Anales de Cuautitlán.*

1. Tezcatlipoca's phrase "make him know his body" refers to making the king conscious of his natural appetites that had been attenuated by his penitence and spiritual exercises.

CHAPTER NINETEEN

THE RABBIT IN THE MIRROR

1 Following this, Tezcatlipoca went to complete his devilry. He assumed the appearance of a very little old man, wrinkled and bent all the way to the ground. He walked toward the royal palace, carrying a mirror wrapped in cloth.[1] The mirror was a double-faced sheet of highly polished obsidian. Making use of his magical arts, the sorcerer conjured the image of a bloodied rabbit in each side of the mirror.[2]

2 When he arrived at the palace he addressed the guards: "Greetings, oh lords. I request that you notify the high priest that an old man has come to give him the knowledge of his own body." To this they answered: "Go away, old man. You cannot see him. He is fasting now and your presence will only make him angry and sad."

3 But Tezcatlipoca was very persistent: "One way or another I must see him!" After much insistence the guardians finally gave in: "Well, wait here while we tell him."

4 Then they went to notify Ce Acatl: "Lord, an old man has come and wishes to see you. We sent him away but he refuses to go, saying that by any means he must see you. He told us that he has come to show you your body."

5 "My body! What is the meaning of that? Search him and see what he has, then let him in."

6 They took this message to the old man and ordered him: "Before entering you must show us what you have. "But he didn't want to. "I didn't come to show it to everyone; it is for his eyes only. Go and tell him that this old man is insisting that it should be me who shows him his face."

7 Again the guards went to the king, taking the old man's answer with them. Finally the king accepted with these words: "Let him in, for he is coming to me. It has been many days that I have awaited a messenger."

8 They called in the old man. He came into the king's presence, greeted him, and said: "My son, priest, I greet you. I am coming to show you your body, your own flesh." Ce Acatl responded: "Be welcomed, grandfather. Where are you coming from? Are you tired? Are you, perhaps, my father's messenger?"

9 Then the old man said: "My son, priest. I come from the mountain of the foreigners. I am your servant, your slave. I am in charge of giving you a message. I have come to show you your image.

10 The prince then asked him: "What is that you say about my image? How is it? Show it to me, let me see it!" Then Tezcatlipoca unwrapped the mirror and gave it to Ce Acatl, saying: "This is your body. Take a good look at it in the mirror. Oh penitent, recognize yourself, for you must see your own shape."[3]

11 Upon looking at himself in the mirror, the king saw the bloody rabbit that Tezcatlipoca had placed there. Then, full of fear, he threw away the mirror, screaming: "Is that how I am? Is it possible that my people see me like that? Could they look at my body without becoming fearful or without making fun of me? I would think that they would run away in fear, for ugly is my aspect, old and wrinkled is my face, sunken are my eyes, swollen is my flesh, and deformed is my figure."

12 Then Ce Acatl became bitter, and after a long silence he said: "Never should my people see me again! Here, without choice, I will remain locked up. I will never see light again. Darkness will be my curtain, and the underground basement of the temple will be my shelter forever. Go away, old man! You have greatly burdened me."[4] Hearing these words, Tezcatlipoca said goodbye and humbly left.

Source for this chapter: *Anales de Cuautitlán.*

1. In this symbolic context, the mirror indicates the personality. This episode alludes to Ce Acatl's exit from the state of abstraction in which his consciousness had resided. The black mirror also represents Tezcatlipoca's role as the Lord of Temptation and of the mysterious initiation.
2. The rabbit is one of Ce Acatl's Nahuals. In this instance it represents his aspect as the god of drunkenness. The animal also represents the moon, which in its turn is the patron deity of the mind and sexuality.
3. Through verbal suggestion Ce Acatl was obliged to identify himself with his reflection.
4. The tempter's strategy had three parts: first, to oblige Ce Acatl to be in touch with his corporeal reality; second, to numb his senses so he could identify with his animal side and forget his divine essence; and third, to provoke in him a reaction of attachment.

CHAPTER TWENTY

THE MAKEUP

1 The rumored news was that the prince would not leave the palace, not even for the business of running the city; he would spend his days wandering in the darkness of its basement. The Toltecs began to demand his presence.

2 The ministers gathered to talk about ways to obligate him to come out of his retreat. Tezcatlipoca, who was attending the meeting in his disguise as a priest, told them: "It is time to call in Omecoyotl, the feather maestro, to prepare the royal makeup."

3 So the foremost feather artisan was notified: "The lord is in need of your services. Go and prepare him to appear in public." To this he answered: "In good time I am going to see him."

4 Then Omecoyotl went to the temple where the king was hiding and addressed him: "Oh, my prince, I suggest that you go out so that your people can see you." But the king answered: "No, because I don't want them to see me and run away scared."

5 Then the artisan insisted: "That can be fixed. I will improve your appearance with makeup and feathers. You will look radiant." He persisted in this way until the king finally gave in, saying: "Well, grandfather, be it as you wish!"

6 Omecoyotl wrapped the king in his feather insignia, put a green mask on his face, and touched his lips with red paint. He put yellow on his cheeks and painted a set of fangs on his mouth. After that he adorned the king's hair and beard with precious feathers and dressed his neck with them. Finally he dressed the king in a fine tunic and sandals.[1]

7 Once all this was done, he brought a mirror. When Ce Acatl saw his reflection he was very happy and he immediately left the rooms where he was hiding. Then Omecoyotl sent a message to the noble ones saying: "Lords, I have done according to your wishes."

8 To this Tezcatlipoca answered: "Excellent! Now I will take charge." So, in collusion with one of his helpers, Toltecatl and Tezcatlipoca started moving, for their time had come.

✱ Source for this chapter: *Anales de Cuautitlán.*

---

1. On the tunic were Tlaloc's insignias. The intention was for him to give the people an image of prosperity.

CHAPTER TWENTY-ONE

DRUNKENNESS

1 Ce Acatl kept a piece of property in Xonapacoyan where the food that was consumed by the court was prepared. His corporal, Maxtlaton, was in charge of the property. Tezcatlipoca and his helper went to the corporal's house and there they spent the night.

2 Maxtlaton had two virgin daughters who were dedicated to the service of Quetzalcoatl. He was very protective of their upbringing. Therefore, when he saw the strangers coming, he locked up his daughters before attending to business. His actions, however, were not hidden from Tezcatlipoca.

3 The travelers asked Maxtlaton for provisions. They took plants, tomatoes, chilies, and corn from which they prepared different dishes. They also asked for agave milk. In only four days they prepared wine and added to it honey from bees and a type of mushroom that induces drunkenness.

4 Toltecatl and Tezcatlipoca both took on the appearance of holy pilgrims and went then to Tula, taking everything with them: the vegetables, the fruits, and the drugged wine. When they arrived at the royal palace, they asked to be admitted, but the guards did not allow it. One, two, three times they came back without being received.

5 Finally the guards asked them where they had come from. And they answered: "We come from the mountain of the wise ones, oh lords, and we bring a present for the penitent." When Ce Acatl heard this message, he gave the order to allow them in.

6 So they entered the royal chambers and, while performing their greetings, offered their presents. The king asked them: "Who are you, grandfathers? Why have you come? Could it be that you have with you a certain answer that I have been expecting for many days?"

7 They answered: "We are the wise ones from the mountain of the wise ones, artisans from the land of art. Oh priest, we have come to give you a message. But before that, you must eat." And they placed before him his present.

8 Ce Acatl had misgivings about eating, but finally he tasted a bite and was very happy. After he had eaten, the pilgrims asked him again: "Drink. We have prepared for you this white nectar. We beg you, drink the wine."

9 But he refused saying: "No, old ones, I will not drink, for I am a fasting penitent and I am not used to it. Perhaps this nectar is deadly or would make me drunk, and my body is thin and weak; my legs can hardly carry me."

10 But they told him: "This, lord, is good medicine. Very healthy and tasty. It gladdens the heart of whoever drinks it." And as Ce Acatl was resisting, they kept on insisting: "At least try it with your little finger and you will see your sadness disappear! It is a good wine."

11 After tasting it with his finger, Ce Acatl was driven to drink, and he told them: "Grandfathers, I will accept three more drinks." But in perfidy they answered him: "Oh priest, you must drink four times, for such is the tradition in our lands."

12 So the king drank and, calling on his servants, he ordered them to drink as well. Four douses they served to each one of them, and then they presented a fifth one begging: "Keep on drinking, in honor of your greatness!" That is how they all drank the wine with mushrooms until they were totally drunk.[1]

❈ Sources for this chapter: *Anales de Cuautitlán* and *Relaciones históricas.*

1. Within the mythological theme of the temptations, Ce Acatl's drunkenness is the equivalent of Satan's proposal to Jesus that the latter throw himself from the temple's roof.

CHAPTER TWENTY-TWO

THE FIELDS OF THE SUN

1 Then Ce Acatl's mind lost consciousness and his body was left in a faint while his ecstatic soul experienced the deepest joy. And in his joy he sang:

2 "Oh lords, I drank your strengthened liquor. My heart delights in tasting the foam of the flowers; my soul is drunk! Oh, my fathers, with the drunkenness from the grass that overtakes the senses, you conquer hearts. Oh, you old ones who have flowers and feather flags! In truth you are the owners of a hidden treasure, oh grandfathers."

3 Toltecatl and Tezcatlipoca answered: "You have been drinking, lord, and have become drunk. Your heart is now without shape, it has been healed. Do you remember now your work and your fatigue, your death and your departure to the world of splendor?"

4 "My death! Oh, old ones, what words are those? Where must I go?" They answered: "Surely you must walk in that country, the world of the black color, the seat of the red color. There, from the beginning of time, an old lord, your true father, awaits you. He will give you the inheritance of a new kingdom, bigger and better than the one you now possess."

5 With the words of the old men, Ca Acatl was greatly surprised. "Oh, grandfathers, what are you talking about? What king is this, and from what kingdom? Why is it so important that I go with him? And once I am there, what will become of my people?"

6 They answered: "Look, prince: That lord is the sun who gives us light and his kingdom is the magic field of the infinite butterflies,[1] where his dancers and musicians continuously praise him. There you will go, and you two will talk with understanding. When you come into his presence you will have a body, then you will be changed from man to a youth to a child."

7 On hearing these words Ce Acatl's heart grew afraid and he said: "Old ones, I don't want to go there. I don't want anymore of your medicine!" But they insisted: "Lord, drink some more. This is god's nectar and if you don't drink it now, later you will suffer a burning desire for it and you will not be able to have it."

8 The king was in doubt, asking himself if, in reality, that was the answer he had been waiting for. But Tezcatlipoca added: "Penitent, your prayers have been heard. I know of your longings. I know how much you wish to go to that faraway land so distant from our own. Because of your longing you live in penitence and lack spark for life."

9 "With the medicine that we gave you, you will finally reach your goal and get the kingdom of your desires, and you will get the necessary strength to set on the great journey. Besides, as a price, you will completely forget all the fatigues and hardships of this life, the illnesses suffered by you and your people, and you will also forget your mortal condition."

10 "It is true, my grandfathers," he answered. "You don't know how much I desire this. It is my burning hope to make myself immortal and set on the journey of eternity. And toward that end I have focused myself in unimaginable attempts."

11 Toltecatl and Tezcatlipoca pleaded again: "Drink some more of the wine, but if you don't want to taste it, at least put some on your forehead."[2] And so he did.

12 When he was completely drunk they told him: "Priest, now sing your song." And these are the words that he sang: "My green house, my house of quetzal feathers, my house of golden feathers, I must abandon the temple of the shells. . . ."[3]

🔯 Sources for this chapter: *Anales de Cuautitlán* and *Romances de los señores de la Nueva España*.

---

1. This refers to the region of the souls.
2. The effect of these mushrooms can take place through the skin. This phrase seems to reveal an ancient practice of entheogenic communion.
3. The house of the green feathers is a symbol of the physical body and the temple of the shells represents human breathing. Here Ce Acatl is talking about his death.

CHAPTER TWENTY-THREE

THE KIDNAPPING OF THE PRINCESS

1 Then Ce Acatl remembered his sister, the princess Quetzalpetatl, who was a penitent in the women's temple.[1] He asked the old men to bring her: "Go and find my elder sister and bring her with you so that together we may drink and sing!"

2 And so they went. Then, after entering the maiden's chambers, Tezcatlipoca blew his breath on Quetzalpetatl and said: "I, myself, whose name is darkness, the one from the nine infernal regions, command you: Come, enchanted dream! Come, sister, into the nine regions![2] I, the dual lord, order it; I, the one who twists my joints;[3]

I, the one who raises my fearsome voice, sending it everywhere!
Sleep!"

3 When the princess was asleep, Tezcatlipoca called his helper:
"Come, priest Ce Tecpatl! You must verify that the princess sleeps
and must take her with you, for she would not love any other man,
nor will she desire any other but her own brother.

4 "Go! Take her to the center of the earth, to the nine depths, and
surround her with darkness so that she will not recognize me, so
that she will not feel anything, even if you move her to each of the
four directions. I, the war, for whom everything is a joke, make fun
of everyone, converting one person into another, making them lose
all sensibility because I am the enemy, the deceiver. When I want
someone, I deliver him drunk into the darkness of dreams."

5 Ce Tecpatl then took Quetzalpetatl by the hand, even though by
doing so he was betraying his obligations. Tamely, she told him: "Be
it as you want, grandfather. Let us go then."[4] And for the guards in
charge of the custody of the house of the maidens, Tezcatlipoca invoked a dream, and they all fell into a deep, lethargic sleep.

> 🔆 Sources for this chapter: *Anales de Cuautitlán* and *Tratado de las
> idolatrías.*

1. Most probably she was a sister on his father's side. The meaning of her name is
   "feather mat," and is a nickname for the goddess of the water.
2. This is a formula for hypnosis. The nine regions are the supra world, the unconscious state.
3. The Nahual who twists his articulations is Xolotl, "the monster," Quetzalcoatl's
   infernal twin whose conventional posture has the shape of a swastika.
4. She is, at this point, in a trance, as if hypnotized.

CHAPTER TWENTY-FOUR

QUETZALPETATL

1 When the princess arrived she greeted Ce Acatl and told him: "Oh, brother, I've come from the jungles of the tiger, from the palace of torments. I am Quetzalpetatl and I am here to perform a song for my lord."

2 He then returned her greeting: "Be joyful, maiden! Fill your laughter with pleasure and your heart with kindness because today is the time of joy for all, the time to give color to our feelings."

3 Then she was assigned a precious mat by the king. She was fed and offered four cups of wine. A fifth one was in honor of her greatness. To give her joy music the old men sang: "Oh, you, Quetzalpetatl, my sister! Where have you gone on the day of your fasting? Forget it, get drunk!"

4 After the king and Quetzalpetatl drank, they lost all power of judgment; they didn't stop to reflect that they were ascetic mystics.

They didn't remember the time of the nocturnal bath, the spines, the mat, the silence, the solitary morning practices . . . nothing.

5 Then Ce Acatl's tongue relaxed and he began to sing: "In the crystalline bosom where desire is born, I yearn for you, woman. I'm tired from the pain of love. Come to my aid attired in your dress of serpents, my divine sister. Truly you are as beautiful as a goddess. I want to have you, not tomorrow nor after tomorrow! Now!

6 "I, the warrior,[1] as bright as the sun, as beautiful as the dawn. Am I, perhaps, a commoner? No! I was born and I have lived because of the flowery feminine sex.[2] In truth you are worth regarding as a goddess, as a mother and sister. You are as beautiful as no other in the world. This desire of love has made me cry. I want you now!"

7 Finally sleep overtook them. Then the sorcerers sang the second part of their song: "See! The one of the turquoise jewels, the blue stones, the man lies here without consciousness. See! He is embracing a woman with his arm."

8 And to scorn Quetzalpetatl they sang their third song: "What have you done, Quetzalpetatl, my elder sister? You, heart of stone, unreachable woman! You, the woman warrior! Have you got a prisoner? Have you captured the son of the gods?"

Sources for this chapter: *Romances de los señores de la Nueva España* and *Tratado de las idolatrías.*

1. This refers to the war of the spines, the ascetic condition.
2. In the Toltec vision, the fact that each person comes from a woman makes existence divine.

CHAPTER TWENTY-FIVE

THE AWAKENING

1 In the morning Tezcatlipoca told his helper: "It is time for them to wake up." Then he came close to them and recited an incantation: "Here, I call you from the center of the world, from the four directions. I call you to break the spell with which I have dominated and transformed you. I call you; come out from the depths of the dream of darkness.

2 "Now I am leaving. Your lord is departing. Come back, I order you to come back from the drunkenness of the night!" Thus they awoke and the sorcerers greeted them and quickly departed.

3 When the princess awoke her face grew somber and she said: "Oh, brother, those precious elders transported us with the white wine of the agave! Where am I? What have we done? I have been in your hands, I, a little bird, a necklace of jades. I am only a woman and you have appreciated me. I wish my heart could be capable of enjoying and welcoming such pleasure! Oh, brother, I came only to sing and you have made me drunk."

4 Ce Acatl complained: "Unfortunate am I! I have sinned. What could I do to go back? How can I clean the stain that I have put on my body?"[1] Then he sent the maiden with her servants to her mother.[2]

5 When she entered the temple, the young maiden prostrated herself and said: "Mother, I am coming from up there, from the palace of the precious stones. There I have been deceived; my soul has been devalued. When I talk to myself I can only think that I am like a woman for sale. My heart is sick from my thoughts. Could it be that those living in abomination will begin to come here? Punish me for it, oh, my mother!"

> ✳ Sources for this chapter: *Romances de los señores de la Nueva España* and *Tratado de las idolatrías*.

1. A theological principle of the Nahuatl doctrine is the humility of the mediator (penitent). It was required that the penitent limit himself totally, including denying himself participation in the human sin of consciousness. This justifies the total effort for redemption. The value of the penitent, or mediator, lies in his example and not in some symbolic transfer of evil. Sin is not seen as an innate human condition but as a result of concrete actions. A redeemer that has not lifted himself up from evil is not understood.
2. Most probably this refers to Quetzalpetatl's spiritual mother, the principal of the temple where the princess lived.

CHAPTER TWENTY-SIX

THE GODDESS OF THE WATERS

1 The news spread rapidly throughout the city, for Tezcatlipoca, with feigned shame, went everywhere, inflaming the people's mood. The neighbors started to murmur insults against Ce Acatl.

2 Meanwhile, in a corner of his chamber and before an image of Chalchiuhtlicue, the penitent was praying: "What would you do with me, oh mother? The one covered with a dress of jades. What would you do with me? Cleanse my human part in some place of whirlwinds, yonder where the currents are deposited, where forever movement flows. Purify me, oh spirit of the air.

3 "Before you I come with my weak parts in pain. Could it be that I don't deserve your compassion? Here are the numbed stone, the drunken stick, and the raped earth. Could it be that you wish to damage your son forever?"

4 Suddenly the image on the wall came to life. Wrapped in her resplendent clothes, the goddess appeared in all her radiance with sounds of crashing currents. Overwhelmed, Ce Acatl fell at her feet. Then the apparition, fixing her eyes on him, said:

5 "My man, you, the owner of a face! How come you are not ashamed of failing your own people? Perhaps you forgot, perhaps your heart ignores that it is me who broke your abstinence? Don't you know that in the chamber of jades you slept with me, with Xochiquetzal?

6 "I came there as a sister. I came to greet you, to congratulate you, and tamely you accepted my human body. I threw my clothes on you, I covered you and wrapped your head with my shirt. And tamed, you slept in my arms!

7 "My man, how come you were not ashamed of being entwined with a human body? Now, because of that, you must go. Yes, you will go. I have come here only to apprehend you, to interrupt your life. Here concludes your power forever. You will not go on!"[1]

✻ Sources for this chapter: *Romances de los señores de la Nueva España* and *Tratado de las idolatrías.*

---

1. As we will later see, the goddess's cruelty is only a facade. Her objective is to exile Ce Acatl in order to universalize his status as a mediator.

CHAPTER TWENTY-SEVEN

THE EXPELLING

1 Scandalized, the chief ministers agreed to put an end to the grievances. They all came to the conclusion that in order to stop Ce Acatl from contaminating the Toltecs with his example, it was necessary to expel him from the kingdom. Tezcatlipoca was the happiest of all with this decision.

2 A herald was sent to the king urging him to come to the chamber of the council. When he arrived, he entered, full of sorrow and with his head down. Chicomexochitl, the spokesman and great minister, intercepted him saying: "Stop, priest! Where have you wounded us? Right in the most intimate place."

3 "Go, out beyond our borders! I, the Minister of Seven Flowers, order you. Quickly go away, you affront to your people! Could it be that your heart has forgotten? You broke your ties there in the turquoise chamber by the altar of the polished stones. There you had your fun, there you became drunk. Now what can you argue?

4 "Go far, without protesting. Go to mock other people! Quietly leave this place, or should we wait until tomorrow or after tomorrow? Leave now, right away. If you don't leave, if you resist, we already know what we will do with you. And you, our Mother Earth, keep him company, make this priest's way more difficult with barriers of fire.

5 Hearing these words, Ce Acatl left the chambers. But the ministers remained in council to determine what to do with the responsibilities of the kingdom. It was agreed to assume power collectively until a successor was found.

6 But Tezcatlipoca was conspiring, persuading some and intimidating others, with the aim of putting on the throne one of his allies, a certain young man named Huemac who was Ce Acatl's relative. Finally, that was what happened.

✳ Source for this chapter: *Tratado de las idolatrías.*

CHAPTER TWENTY-EIGHT

THE COFFIN

1 On leaving the council's chambers, Ce Acatl wandered all through the royal house in a detached farewell visit with all the things he loved. When he arrived in his dwellings, he found there a number of his servants and friends who had come to console him. Full of shame, he looked at them for a long while. Finally, breaking the silence, he told them:

2 "Sad and desolate is my heart, oh grandfathers. Look at this miserable child, scattering himself as a cloud. I walked through the gardens, went into the chambers. Lords and nobles were adorning themselves with flowers. But here I am, the broken child, scattered as a feather fan thrown to the wind.

3 I drank the wine from the mushrooms and my heart is tormented.

I feel alone in the middle of the earth. I fall into meditation and I see that there is no joy, that I am not happy. Only death and suffering are all around. What else is there for me to do? Truly nothing more, but to die.

4 "Oh you, my friends, my relatives! Even though in this world we were united as a crown of flowers, and furthermore, we were like beads in the same necklace, in truth we are all alone."

5 Then he gave orders for them to prepare a coffin, but as his helpers refused to obey, he asked them: "Friends, this is enough. I must leave this earth. I must die. Bring for me the stone coffin."[1]

6 Thus promptly they brought the coffin. The penitent lay down in it and asked them to put on the lid. With this he prepared the departure of his spirit, in case some god would want to take it. There inside the coffin he rested for four days, his friends guarding him.

7 After this time had passed and seeing that death was not attending his call, he rose, his voice exclaiming: "How should I go, how should I enter Ometeotl's world? It is difficult! What is the road to our communal house? There, where the ones who have defeated their bodies are resting. And here I have been abandoned with all my sadness.

8 Could it be that there is life on the road leading to peace? Is it possible that my heart believes it? You are entrapping us in a coffin, oh giver of life, you gag men with knots of fear. You obligate them even though no one is expecting them. You have abandoned us in the company of our uncertainty."

9 Then, screaming, he said: "Divinity, power, listen to my voice! No one is in my silence! Deities, I invoke you, hear me! No one hears my voice." On hearing his call his servants took him out of the coffin.

Sources for this chapter: *Cantares de los señores de la Nueva España; Anales de Cuautitlán;* and *Chilam Balam de Chumayel.*

1. The coffin is a symbol for change or for a step in an initiation. Its symbolism is equivalent to that of the Christian rite for baptism.

CHAPTER TWENTY-NINE

THE FAREWELL

1 Intending to lead the life of a wanderer in strange lands, Ce Acatl resolved to leave forever the city and the kingdom. Then he wrote the words that he sang to bid goodbye to Tula:

2 "A day of bad accounting was in my house. Let the hearts of the ones absent from here be moved. This is something difficult and dangerous. Only the ones with a body of earth should remain. I wasn't born to be a servant for cheap, coarse works!"

3 While he was singing, all his servants and friends were deeply moved and joined him as he sang. "In no stranger's house has my lord ever been sad. The feathered serpent does not wear anymore her hair of precious stones. What has happened? Meanwhile, perhaps in some place the wood will remain pure? But now, here, let's be sad."

4 And they sang again: "Ah, Quetzalcoatl, our prince! Your name will never be lost. This house of jades will be left standing alone. You will leave alone this house of serpents erected in the city. We desire to cry. Quetzalcoatl, our prince, your name will never be forgotten."

5 Then he said to them: "That is enough, grandfathers! I am leaving. We are leaving. I will find the motive for which my sister cried yesterday. When I find what I am searching for, I will take it. I will follow the wide road, the one that is divided in two, the one that has neither beginning nor end. I will search, I will call. Not tomorrow, or after tomorrow, but now, right away! And I am gone."

6 He then gave instructions regarding his properties: "Hide forever all the richness that we have discovered, close it up from every side. Lay down a screen over our lives to block any memory of us."[1] Thus they did.

7 They hid the most valuable things in the precinct of the ablutions, near the aqueduct. All the things made of silver and coral they buried in the slopes of the mountains. All the books that they could not carry with them were burned. All the marvelous pieces of art, Toltec art, everything, he hid in the secret places where it all still remains.[2]

8 Then he released the precious birds that he kept in his house so that they could fly in the sky. And he asked them to go on ahead of his departure, to go on and wait for him yonder, by the edges of the great waters.

9 And playing a reed flute, he sang the final words of his song: "Not too far back, my mother was still carrying me on her bosom. She was never the courtesan of a god! Today I cry."

Sources for this chapter: *Anales de Cuautitlán; Tratado de las idolatrías; Historia general de las cosas de la Nueva España;* and *Códice Florentino.*

1. This refers to spiritual wealth, to the esoteric knowledge that was not permitted to be diffused.
2. This act is not due to selfishness but is a symbol of detachment from material possessions.

CHAPTER THIRTY
AT THE OUTSKIRTS OF TULA

1 After leaving Tula Ce Acatl stopped to rest with his friends. Many had gone with him to bid him goodbye. He asked them all to return home except for a small group of servants that was always with him.

2 There was also a group of people incited by Tezcatlipoca to insult him and accelerate his departure. They were violent to Ce Acatl's followers, throwing stones at them and laughing. Ce Acatl's friends came to him to ask in what manner they should respond to such violence.

3 He answered, "Haven't I asked myself that question? Unrest overwhelms my spirit. Where is our shelter? Where is our best friend? Is there something on this earth that will not perish? The one for whom we all live seems to be getting tired. Do not let your hearts be tormented. Friends, do not resist anyone. Do not make me restless anymore. In truth, I hardly have any mind left." He then ordered the march to continue.

4 Among his followers was the young man named Huemac, who had the role of a messenger. On seeing him about to depart, Ce Acatl addressed him: "Stop, my friend! Where are you going? This world is the house of the victims. You are only at the door while I am already in the weapon's chamber! Do not go on; remain here. I am being sent far away, alone. I have been taken prisoner, like a duck. I must go far away, but they are following the trail of this miserable duck. Ah, they indulge the sharp blade."

5 In that moment an elder priest came to him and said: "Get moving, our brother! Don't you remember that in the black-colored land, in the seat of the red color, you are expected? There you will find peace." On hearing this advice, Ce Acatl left.

⊛ Source for this chapter: *Cantares de los señores de la Nueva España.*

PART THREE

Only in this way will you know
that you are Toltecs:
If you personally try to get to know
The perfume of incense and the
color of flowers.
Make yourselves Toltecs:
men of self-experience.

CHAPTER ONE

WEEPING OVER TULA

1 And that is how the exodus of Ce Acatl, prince of Tula, began. His servants were with him, taking the precious legacy of Toltec art: the rattles, the drums, the jewels, and the books, and whatever else they could carry with them. They were playing their flutes on their march.

2 Along the way on the journey they found an elevated place where there were some large rocks. There they stopped to rest for the night. The penitent climbed a rock to sit at the top. While he was climbing he put his hands on the face of the rock. The elders relate that in that place you can still see his handprints.

3 From there, far on the horizon, the city of Tula was visible; the torches were beginning to illuminate it. When the penitent saw this, he was moved and exclaimed: "How deserted your patios and your orchards will be! How your dwellings will be emptied! Oh Tula, city of the straight word, you will be left an orphan.

4 "Your palaces of precious woods will be left solitary. Your *Calmecas*[1] of carved columns will be silent. Your pavements of turquoise will be broken, and the temple of the serpents will not be finished. When the people see you they will say: 'He is gone, our prince has abandoned the city! Oh Tula, center of the earth, you will be left an orphan.'"

5 While saying this he could not contain his tears; he was shaken by great sobbing, a double trail of tears as thick as hail spilled down his face. His tears rolled down, drilling the core of the stone. And the elders claim that there where they fell, even today, one can see their marks.

6 So hands and tears were left there clearly printed as if they were pressed in mud, as if the stone had softened so that it could be stamped. There, even today, the hollow spaces can be seen, and because of it, the place is called the Mountain of the Stamp.[2]

⬡ Sources for this chapter: *Códice Florentino; Historia general de las cosas de la Nueva España;* and *Relaciones históricas.*

1. A *calmeca* is a monastery, made up of individual cells.
2. The word *stone* in Nahuatl was the glyph for the creation power and for the nerve nodules in the spinal column. The creation power was activated by the emotional state of the penitent.

CHAPTER TWO
THE NAHUAL

1 Exhausted by the journey of the day, his servants were sleeping. He meditated throughout the night on the latest events until by early dawn he was overcome by exhaustion. Then he took his mat, extended it over the ground, and spoke to it:

2 "My mat, my tiger mat, you that open your mouth toward the four directions, for you are as hungry and thirsty as I am, I conjure you. Should the perverse one dare to come near us, the cheater of men, the agent of bad counsel, protect me, wake me up. Don't you see how lonely and poor I have been left? How senseless I live in this total misery?"[1] Saying this, he lay down on the mat and slept.

3 Then in his dream his Nahual[2] appeared and told him: "My heart, are you complaining? Perhaps you believe that you will remain forever on this earth? Are you anguished? Have you been born or are you your own friend wanting to live only for yourself? And do you feel compassion for yourself?"

4 To this the penitent responded: "Oh, my Nahual, my own heart! Be you a god for me! Make me in your own image, give me your strength, and bring joy to my life. Be my god! Where am I going? My life as been cut from the earth.

5 "Precious is my life for me. I exist. As a singer I was spreading gold and garlands. And there I have to leave the house where I was living. The columns, correctly lined up, are being left there. By any chance have I taken feathers and jades as a prize? Loneliness is my prize.

6 "I was known. I had friends I loved. The time has come for leaving everything. Could I leave to someone my soul as a souvenir? In solitude I am departing, with my heart covered with thorns. Everything has been lost: the feathers, the jades, the paintings, things made with beauty. All of it has been lost! I am leaving and in no place in the world will I find my ideal or my role model."

7 Then his Nahual took him by the hand, showed him the eastern horizon, and told him: "Stop pondering, oh my heart. There, in the place of the final accounting, in the place where, without rage and suffering, the perfect life is lived, is there, perhaps, any memory? Stand up, my heart! Look toward the region of the thorns, to the direction where light is born. There the bonfire and divine water are expecting you. There you will find the power and the kingdom, the beautiful flower."

⬢ Sources for this chapter: *Tratado de las idolatrías* and *Cantares de los señores de la Nueva España.*

1. In this instance the mat represents God. This prayer to the place of dreams or meditation was common among the people of Mesoamerica.
2. The Nahual is like our own twin, our own in-dreaming image. The Nahual's words were considered to be very meaningful because they came from our own subconscious.

CHAPTER THREE
THE CROSSROADS

1 The next day the road took them to a crossroads. Several ways met there, going to the four directions. The one going south penetrated the mountains. Ce Acatl and his pages felt tired and decided to spend the night there.

2 The pages began an argument. Some were proposing to go around the mountains, following a stable road; others wanted to go over the mountains; and some of them wanted to go back to some town or city to find food. They could not agree on what course to take; there was dissension among them. Seeing this, the penitent spoke up, telling them:

3 "Comrades, priests, warriors, I ask you: where should we go? What road should we take? Truly our destiny is uncertain. Grandfathers, friends, I warn you: The flower of our badge eventually will wither; we have it only on loan! And nobody will stop to see how it fades!

4 "They asked us to move aside and make room for others on this earth. We have been left alone at the crossroads. They have thrown us into doubt and discord. We are here only on loan!

5 "Before us the road to wisdom turns rugged, and you are thinking of going back on foot? Think about it, friends, nowhere on this earth will we find rest. Choose the direction that you find to your liking."

6 He then retreated to the forest to find an answer in his prayers. He struggled all night long. Toward the eighth hour a vision came to him: A very skinny little man with his body covered in ashes silently came close to him and said:

7 "Cheer up, walker! You, the tormented one, you with a wounded heart, what are you gaining with it? Reflect: We come to this place only to dwell in sorrow. If we die, isn't it preferable? Face your destiny.

8 "Even if your friends abandon you and your warriors insult you, think: What do you want to do? Do it! Do you want to take another direction? Do it! Take it and go to the place of pain, to the battlefield where the brave ones achieve victory. That is the prize for living on this earth."

✸ Source for this chapter: *Cantares de los señores de la Nueva España.*

CHAPTER FOUR

SONG OF TIMAL

1 Next morning Ce Acatl gathered his pages and told them: " I am leaving, I am going home."

2 Then Timal, the imitator, also spoke: "I will go too! I will go into the country. I will drill the mountains. I will grow to know the seat of wisdom." Then, taking his drum, he sang his farewell words:

3 "Timal, Timal! I have lived, I, the warrior prince. Timal, the exact copy of the venerated elder of the nocturnal serpent. My mother is the one butterfly of stone, my father is the solar being.

4 "I ask my god: Where am I going? I, the foreigner. Who do I follow? What would become of me? But my inner self screams: I want to go too, and penetrate deeply! Wherever the penitent goes, I want to go too!

5 I, Timal, will enhance the creator of the world, there in the place of the eagles, in the place of the tigers.[1] To the far-off land I will go; I will become a wanderer; I will be a foreigner. For my inner self is claiming: I want to go too, I want to delve deeply!"

6 When they heard Timal's song, Ce Acatl's comrades became eager to continue their trip. Then the penitent ordered their steps and assigned Matlaxochitl, the eldest of them all, to watch over them.

🔯 Source for this chapter: *Códice Aubin.*

---

1. These metaphors mean "on the path of the heroic work."

CHAPTER FIVE

IN THE FOUNTAIN

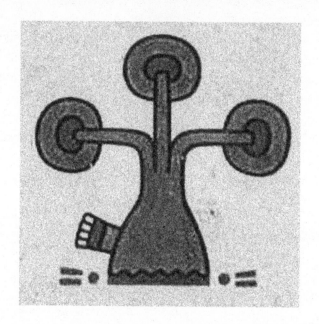

1 They walked on many journeys toward the country of wisdom. One day they came to a place where a spring was flowing near the place where some hermits were living. Because of this, the fountain was called the Spring of the Serpents.[1] There they stopped.

2 The pages were entertaining themselves with music and chanting, but Ce Acatl went into a nearby forest to meditate. Once there, the hermits of the place came to tempt him. They were naked and very thin, a sorry sight to see. Ostentatiously, they displayed their marks of numerous austerities.

3 With kind words they greeted the prince, asking him: "Where are you heading to, young prince? Why have you run away unto these deserted lands, abandoning your city? Could it be that your heart is bored with the earth?"

4 He answered them: "I am not running away, old men, for I have been summoned. My father's messengers showed me the way, and I am going south, to the land of wisdom."

5 They asked him again: "Once you get there, what will you do? Could it be that you will find in other lands what you couldn't reach in your own kingdom?"

6 He answered them: "Old men, I am searching for knowledge. I am going to bring water to my channel. I'm going to place myself before the face of the water.[2] I am going to disrupt the earth, to disrupt heaven. Lords, I am going to war, there where our mother gives colors to our heroes.

7 "I am looking for the colors of the tiger, for the trembling of the eagle in the battlefield. I am searching for the flower of the beasts there, where it blooms, there before the face of the water where an obsidian butterfly flies. I am searching for the place where the one for whom we all live takes those whom he wants. And the one whom he takes he recognizes and makes his own. I am going south, searching for wisdom."

8 Again the hermits came to tempt him: "A great and beautiful kingdom you had there. But yonder, what would you find? Could it be that you are going to forget all that you lived? Will you renounce your fight and duty? Reflect, oh you walker: Who's now going to sustain your people, your city? Who will make penitence for their sins? Who will defend the movement of peace against the infidels? Who will be like a bulwark when the demons grow hungry? Do you already want to give up?"

9 Ce Acatl answered them: "Enough, old men! There is no way that I will go back. I must go on."

10 Seeing his resolve, they blessed him. "Very well, go in good time and may the gods grant you success. But before you go, you must leave here all your culture and art; it is not possible that you take it where you want to go."

11 They asked him for everything: the skills to do the stonework and woodwork, the art to cast silver and work with feathers, the knowledge to compose books and paint characters. He left their jewels. The hermits kept everything.

12 Ce Acatl went back to his followers and told them: "Friends, listen to me. It is necessary that we leave behind our culture. Jades and feathers cannot enter the house of mystery. Rid yourselves, then, of your beautiful jewels, your rattling bells and garlands, and even get rid of your clothes. Loosen your hair and present yourselves just as you came into this world—as unpolluted, virgin children."

13 Obeying, they threw every item of the Toltec inheritance into the fountain. These rapidly sank into the water. Since then it has been called the water of precious jewels.[3]

(✱) Sources for this chapter: *Historia de las indias; Cantares de los señores de la Nueva España;* and *Chilam Balam, libro de los libros.*

---

1. The serpent was a symbol for wisdom, which was an attribute often associated with hermits.
2. Water symbolizes cosmic power, while the channel in this instance represents the human being and the face of the water indicates the supreme consciousness. To place yourself before the face of the water is to deliver your being to the infinite.
3. The jeweled fountain represents an area of the neck that is the access to the wisdom centers. Selfish interests cannot flow through this point.

CHAPTER SIX
THE FROST

1 Before arriving in the country of wisdom, they went through a pass in the mountains called the Smoking Mountain and the Resplendent Woman in the Mother Sierra.[1] The night was cold and it snowed, and because they were tired and naked, some of them found death. That was the final price that the sorcerers had asked: the life of the people.

2 At dawn Ce Acatl saw the frozen bodies of his musicians, his comedians, and the singers that had come with him. Full of grief, he kneeled among the bodies and cried out: "You, who alone there in the most intimate part of heaven, have pronounced sentence. Are you perhaps familiar with the price of life? You, who in your shrine of eternity grow tired with this dream of one day, how come you don't tire of making us cry?"

3 Then he gave orders to bury the bodies. After that he gathered the survivors and promised them: "Friends, do not fear. From now on I will not cause you any more pain. I will not let you be contaminated or covered by shadows. For you have suffered too much with me. You have toiled intensely. Will I forget you? Will I erase you?"

Sources for this chapter: *Historia general de las cosas de la Nueva España* and *Cantares de los señores de la Nueva España.*

1. This location does not refer to geographical limits, but rather to esoteric ones. Both mountains represent the two points in the throat that are guarding the passage of breath. In the physiological code, the country of wisdom is the head. Geographically, it is the Mayan kingdom.

CHAPTER SEVEN
HIS FOLLOWERS

1 Year Two Acatl (987 C.E.). Only eight people entered the country with him: Timal, also called the imitator; Ocelotl, Ozomatl, Cuauhtli, Huitzilo, Chicomecoatl, Xiuhcoatl, and Matlaxochitl, who, being the eldest, also had the most authority.

2 These men who were dedicated to Ce Acatl's service went everywhere as the keepers of his word, dutifully spreading it throughout the country. After he left them, they scattered themselves around the world, telling the news of his deeds.

3 Ce Acatl commended these men to a penitent's life, living in community and retired from the multitudes. He also asked them to be chaste and to practice regular fasting. He asked them, as well, not to forget the things they learned in Tula, but to remember them and share them.

4 When they entered the southern land, they adopted pilgrims' robes: the dresses called Miccatilma and Moztlacaquetza.[1] They let their beards and hair grow long and wore neither hats nor sashes nor adornments. And as a shield, the penitent introduced a wooden necklace to be used for their prayers. This was called Tzoactli or Motoloni.[2]

5 He walked everywhere and was generally welcomed, for the news of his expulsion from Tula and the stalking and ambush of the sorcerers flew before him and was well known. One by one, the number of his followers grew so that when he arrived in the city of the Itzaes, they numbered about four hundred people.

🏵 Sources for this chapter: *Historia de las indias* and *Códice Florentino.*

1. "Blanket of the dead" and "radiant tunic," respectively. The first dress, which was black, was only used by the priests. The second was white and was used by anyone in the community.
2. "The accepted one" and "the poor one," respectively. This simple, humble necklace represented the ones who were absent from the ceremonies. It was not the property of any individual but rather belonged to the temple. It was used in a way very similar to the Christian rosary.

CHAPTER EIGHT

IN THE KINGDOM OF THE SOUTH

1 The inhabitants of Chichen Itza welcomed him with great ceremony, for they said that the penitent, as the king of Tula, had power to heal. Many sick would come to his retreat to be touched by him. The elders say that he healed many people there.

2 The news of his presence traveled everywhere, for the memory of his kingdom was a positive one. Many kings came to see him, asking for advice and counsel. Many others sent their ambassadors to learn from him the arts and the ways of the Toltec government. Others came to invite him to visit their kingdoms or to ask that he send an ambassador to their dominion.

3 On Cozumel, an island that is close to firm land, he had a shrine made of limestone and quarry stone. It was ten measurements high in the middle of a much painted and decorated patio. He also had a very solemn temple built where many devotees were constantly in attendance. On the shrine he put a cross in memory of the sons of Tlaloc, the lords of the four directions, and he left it there so the inhabitants would remember his passing though their place.[1]

4 His followers came to be so many that the lords of the land asked him to establish himself in an independent city. He then chose a park close to the city that they called Tiho.[2] There he had a very good foundation made as the base for his campsite. Encircling this base was a wall as thick as an eighth of a league, leaving two narrow doors as the only access to the city.

5 In the patio they built temples in remembrance of the ones in Tula. The biggest one they named the Temple of the Feathered Serpent. They made another one, round with four doors and different from any other building in these lands, which was dedicated to the cult of the spirit.[3] They also built houses for themselves and a court for the ball game where Ce Acatl and his friends would exercise.

6 He established that the lords of those lands would gather periodically in his citadel to talk about the business of the kingdom and make agreements on peace councils. Up until then the kingdoms of the land had been divided, but by the time he went away, everyone was enjoying a great deal of peace and friendship.

7 He advised the lords to go through towns and cities and find the blind and the lame in order to provide them with whatever they needed. He also advised them to look after the education of the children and the welfare of the elders and the poor. He suggested that they find skillful people for government service and appoint them with the tasks of looking after the children and the peace of the town. He asked them to work hard for themselves and their people.

8 In the city of the Itzaes he searched for the wise men, to learn from their wisdom. And they entrusted him with all their secrets and consoled him for all the tribulations he had suffered since Tula.

9 And there the Cacchiqueles came looking for him to ask him to be their king. But he refused and recommended instead Timal, his disciple.[4] After Ce Acatl left Itzaes, Timal fulfilled that commitment and went with them and founded a dynasty of kings and priests. Also the *pipiles*[5] came looking for Ce Acatl, asking to be acknowledged. He went with them to establish the borders of their kingdom.

10 Wherever he went, he left some of his disciples to represent him and to transmit the Toltec ways.[6] In turn, in each place he searched for knowledge among the elders and the wise ones and studied their beliefs, customs, and ways of life. That is how he perfected his own wisdom.[7]

✳ Sources for this chapter: *Códice Florentino* and *Anales de los Cakchikeles*.

---

1. The cross named after Saint Andrew (a saltire, or x-shaped cross) was the symbol of Quetzalcoatl's religion.
2. Now called Merida.
3. These temples had a floor in the shape of the ansate cross, which is the symbol of life.
4. Information on the kingdom of Timal is in the *Annals of the Cakchikeles*.
5. The *pipiles* were the governors of Nicaragua.
6. As the Popol Vuh narrates, Quetzalcoatl's disciples were also governors of the Quiches from Guatemala.
7. It is possible that the activities of Quetzalcoatl's disciples reached all the way to the high cultures of the Andes, for the people there worshiped a feathered serpent called Viracocha, "seed of the ocean."

CHAPTER NINE

THE WELL

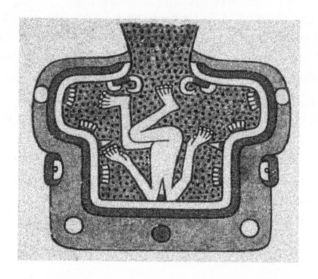

1 Year Six Acatl (992 C.E.). The elders narrate that Tezcatlipoca did send his accomplices to follow Ce Acatl, to spy on his activities, and to hamper his way, using intrigues and manipulations. And some of the vile men from the region rose up against him and tried to assassinate him. But Ometeotl was guiding his steps and he always managed to escape untouched from those who stalked him. Then the sorcerers planned another scheme.

2 There was in this city a well that was famous for its sacredness. Pilgrims from every region of the earth came to bring offerings and to take some of its waters. Ce Acatl developed the routine of coming down every morning to the mouth of the well to meditate on his good and bad actions, on the sense of his steps, and on the designs of the heavens.

3 One day Tezcatlipoca's men appeared by the well and threw a child into the waters. In this way they drowned two or three children. And then the people began to talk about it.

4 Such deeds filled Ce Acatl's heart with fear. Taking these actions as Ometeotl's signal, he resolved that it was time to move his campsite and continue on his way. Therefore, he gathered his friends in a farewell reunion, asking them to remain loyal to his memory, and then he left.

5 On his way back to the Toltec kingdom he stopped in Champoton. Near there, out in the sea, only at a stone's throw from land, he had built an edifice for himself. In this way Ce Acatl left perpetual memory of himself in the kingdom of the south.

❀ Sources for this chapter: *Descripcion de las cosas de Yucatan* and *Relaciones históricas.*

CHAPTER TEN

IN CHOLULA

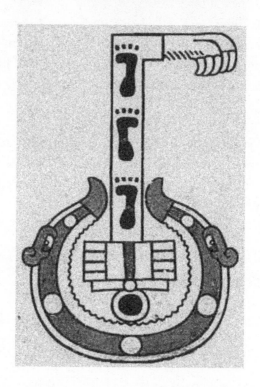

1 On his journey he passed the city of Tenayuca, where he remained for some time. After that he went to Culhuacan and remained there for a while. From there he crossed the mountains and went up to Cuauhquecholan, where the natives erected in his name a temple and a shrine in which they worshiped him as a god. They also asked him to name Matlaxochitl as his ambassador.

2 The pilgrims suffered great hardships, for the kingdom was divided. Its inhabitants had forgotten Ometeotl's law and, siding with Tezcatlipoca's party, had begun to pay tribute to the enemies of Tula. Everywhere the ministers of the sorcerer were marching, using promises and treasures to seduce the people and force them to follow.

Towns and even families were divided, each individual worshiping whomever they thought better. There was much confusion among the people.

3 In the midst of all this contamination the city of Cholula remained pure, for within its limits the memory of Quetzalcoatl was strong. Many ministers of the ancient law, harassed and vexed by the accomplices of the sorcerer, sought shelter in that city and established a good government there. It was to Cholula, then, that the penitent directed his steps.

4 When he arrived in the city, he was so well received that he decided to establish himself permanently with the Cholutecs. They, in their turn, erected for him a magnificent, well-constructed, and beautiful temple. They also offered him the use of some caves close to the temple, where he took refuge with his people.

5 In Cholula Ce Acatl began to spread his teachings in concordance with the signals and voices from heaven, making use of all the things he learned as a pilgrim throughout the lands he had traveled in and his learning with the wise ones of the south.

Sources for this chapter: *Teogonía e historia de los Mexicanos* and *Descripcion de las cosas de Yucatan.*

CHAPTER ELEVEN

THE TEACHINGS

1 And these are the words with which Ce Acatl instructed the Cholultecs: "God is one, Quetzalcoatl is his name. He does not demand anything; he does not need anything. But you should offer him butterflies and serpents, only that."[1]

2 And he told them: "Our parents and grandparents taught us that he shaped and created us, he whose creatures we are, our lord Quetzalcoatl. He also created the heavens, the sun, and the divine earth. Keep it present.

3 "In truth, this is how it is. For whatever is due to him, and because of his sacrifices, he created men and made of us human beings. In this way he came to be Quetzalcoatl, lord and lady of all duality, precious twin. And that is how he transmitted his breath and his word."[2]

4 And he told them: "The heavens are thirteen and the many steps are the journeys.[3] There he is, there is where the true god dwells, the one of two shapes, the being from heaven, lord and lady of duality. The one that is Ometeotl is ruler over the thirteen heavens.

5 "From there we receive life, we, the deserving ones. And from there, when a little child slips through and gets into our inner being, our destiny falls if it is rightly placed. There is the origin of our being and our faith, for so the god of duality has ordered. For he said it, he ordered for himself, and because of that we exist. Do not forget it, either in the day or in the night; invoke him in your sigh and in affliction."

6 And he told them: "The Toltec is wise, he is a luminary, a torch, a great smokeless torch. He imprints wisdom on other people's faces, he makes them take heart. He never misses anything. He stops, observes, and reflects.

7 "The true Toltec, the disciple, is abundant, diverse, restless, capable, and skillful. He is a self-made man who teaches himself, talks with his own heart, finds answers within himself.

8 "The true Toltec gets everything from his heart; he acts with pleasure taking his time to make things; he is careful. As an artist, he is a skillful composer. He creates, fixes whatever is broken, and gathers whatever has been dispersed, making things match.

9 "On the contrary, the false Toltec acts haphazardly and is a disappointment to the people. He darkens everything; he steps on the face of things. He is careless; he does not create. He is an imitator, a fraud, and a thief.

10 "Do become Toltecs, men of self-experience. If you acquire the habit and the discipline of consulting your own heart for everything, you will become Toltecs.

11 "Study the stars, their names and influences, and practice that knowledge. Learn how the sky is moving, how it turns around. Get to know the length of the year and its signs. Learn how the moons march in due order: eighteen moons and here comes the harvest cycle once again.[4] Also learn how long it takes for the harvesting of men, the human gestation: thirteen moons, each in the right order, and then comes the birthing. And learn the measurements for the life span of a man.[5]

12 "Learn the glyphs and the words. Sing and speak well. Have good conversations, give good answers, and offer good prayers. The word is not something that you can buy.

13 "Know the honorable condition, and that it is good. Do not commit adultery; do not become drunk; do not deliver yourself immoderately to gambling nor subjugate yourself to chance; do not mention your lineage nor your virile condition; do not be indiscrete or cowardly; do not strive for first place.

14 "Avoid extremes; keep yourself in the middle, for only in the middle exists the social condition, the honorable condition. Then you will become Toltecs."

15 And he told them: "The wise one is a light, a torch, a mirror drilled on both sides.[6] His are the black and red inks and his are the codices. He himself is writing and wisdom, a true pathway for others; he leads people and things and is an authority on human affairs.

16 "The true wise one is careful, keeps the tradition, and holds the transmission of the doctrine. He teaches it to others; he follows the truth. He is a teacher.

17 "A true teacher never ceases to admonish; that is how he makes other people's faces wise; he makes us to take a face and develop it; he opens our ears and illuminates us. He is a teacher of teachers; he offers a path. We depend on him.

18 "He places a mirror before the others. He makes them sane and careful and makes an identity appear on them. He looks upon everything he does; he regulates his way, arranges everything, and makes order. He shines his light over the world. That is the reason he knows that which is over us and the region of the dead.

19 "Thanks to him we are all comforted, corrected, and taught. Because of him the child humanizes his wants and receives a strict education. He comforts people's hearts, he helps, and he cures and heals everyone."

20 "On the other hand, the false wise one is like a doctor who ignores his trade, or like a man without sanity. He says that he knows about God, that he knows the tradition and keeps it. But that is only vainglory; he only has vanity. He makes things difficult; he is boastful; he is inflated; he is a torrent, a rocky ground.

21 "A lover of darkness and corners, he is a mysterious "wise one," a wizard with secrets, a dreamer who steals from his public because he takes something that is theirs. He is a sorcerer: He twists other people's faces and loses them; he makes others lose identity. He is false: Instead of making things clear, he hides them; he makes things more difficult; he destroys them. Those who follow him perish because of the strength of his mysteries. He finishes with everything."

22 And he told them: "Now get to know the medicine man. The true doctor is a wise one. He gives life; he knows herbs, stones, trees, and roots from personal experience. He has practiced his remedies. He examines, experiments, heals sickness, gives massages, fixes bones, and purges people. He makes them feel better by giving them brews, bleeding them, cutting them, and sewing them. He makes them react and covers them with ashes.

23 "On the other hand, the false doctor mocks his peers, and in his gibe he kills people with medicines. He provokes indigestion, makes illnesses worse, and hides in his secrets, for he is a sorcerer.

He possesses malefic seeds and herbs; he is a wizard, a diviner, a fortune-teller; he kills with his remedies; he makes things worse and casts spells with seeds and herbs.

24 "And the true father, the roots and beginning of men's lineage, is good of heart; he receives things, is compassionate, and cares for everything. Precision is his, his support. With his hands he protects. He raises and educates the children; he teaches and admonishes them; he gives them examples to live by; he places before them a great mirror drilled on both faces. He is a thick, smokeless torch.

25 "And here comes the mature man, a full person with a firm heart like a rock, a wise face. He is owner of his face and heart. Skillful and understanding, a good text composer, he is a Toltec of the black and red inks; he is intelligent. God is in his heart and with his heart he knows things; he talks with his own heart.

26 "And the true artist is a man with the knowledge of colors. He applies them; he knows about shades and harmony; he draws feet, faces, shadows; he achieves effects. As a Toltec he paints the colors of all flowers."

27 Ce Acatl sat down to exhort the citizens of Cholula and told them: "It is good if you support yourselves. Create, work, gather firewood, farm the land, grow edible cactuses. With all that you create, you will drink and you will clothe yourselves. Therefore, honor and enhance hard work. But beware of mundane works, for that which sickens, torments, fatigues, and provokes fear grows fast and fattens rapidly.

28 "How good if by your side the positive word is spoken, the word that causes no harm. If you transmit it, do not enhance or diminish it; say only the exact word. But beware of empty and distracted words. For those only provoke perversion. They are not serene, straight words. The one who speaks them falls into a vacuum; the words take him into a trap to be tied up with a rope, to be stoned, and beaten with a stick.

29 "Get close to the ceiba and to the willow; get close to the one who is a role model and a good example, to the one who is a paragon and signal, black and red, book and painting. Get close to the honorable man of good reputation, to the social condition, to the light, to the torch, to the mirror. Get close to he who everywhere excels, gives light, lives in a way that is good and prudent, joyful and serene, who goes about creating order. Get closer to the ones who are box and coffer, shade and good shelter—thick ceiba, sprouting willow that rises up straight and powerful.

30 "You will not forget those who did not sleep; those who did not hide in dreams; those who did not tear down their lips;[7] those who in peace carry on their legs, arms, and backs the one who amuses himself with dirt and sleeps in the small net, and goes around playing, and drags himself about.

31 "You will not forget the elders, the poor, the suffering, the unhappy ones; the ones with stuck intestines; the ones who have not found home and are living in confusion; the ones who are shedding tears and biting their fingernails; the ones with their hands tied to their backs.

32 "Nor will you forget the ones who walk in pain where the wild beasts dwell and where the mountain turns into walls; the ones who live in the jails of misery and poverty; the ones in the deserts and mountains who, exhausted, go in search of salt, vegetables, spice and water; the ones in plazas who are tricked; the ones with dry lips.

33 "On the other hand, move away from banquets, the river, and the road. Do not stop there, for there the great devourer dwells, the other man's woman, the other woman's man, prosperity, another person's skirt and shirt.

34 "Do not search excessively for a good appearance. For silently he will take you as you are, in any place, at any moment. Your adornments and jewels could throw you into the torrent. Instead, he should see you as one who teaches and cares for things, for the one who is a teacher opens the way for others to escape the vicious circle."

35 And he told them: "Think about it: There is one who lives in drunkenness, saliva falling on his hands. He has stained his neck and his hands, he is quick to defame, and he takes other people's things. He screams and talks by himself, for the herb[8] and the wine have him tied. He does not hold the stone and the stick; he is falling. He does not go out through his own exit; he does not live his own life; he does not run his own race; he no longer has a face or ears; he does not sing or say things; he does not express anything. At the time of the scream he does not scream.

36 "That one has no way and does not know order. He does not pay any attention to the good word that elevates speaker and listener and expresses meaning. He lives without reflection, continuously running away and suddenly falling. Alone, broken, smeared with his own filth—that is how he lives.

37 "That one does not awaken in peace, nor does he go to sleep in joy. He is restless as a rabbit and runs away like a deer. He lives in blindness and is never free from it. He does not want to grow any more. His only wish is to run away; he rejects with his foot. He does not understand anything; he does not retain anything; he is not docile. He throws himself against himself; he indulges in doubt; he strikes, roars, and bites at those around him.

38 "He broke Quetzalcoatl's Law. He does not extend his arm when he must extend it; he will not go where he must go; he is not entering where he must enter; he will not die when he must die. Do not follow those footsteps."

39 Ce Acatl used to sit on the stairs of the great temple of Cholula to teach the Toltec ways. People from all over the city and from other regions would come to him to learn.

40 "Love one another; help one another. Help those in need with a blanket, a truss, a jewel, a salary, food. For it is false to reject those around you.

41 "Give alms to the hungry, even if you have to give your own food. Clothe the one in rags, even if you have to go naked. Help the one who needs you, even if you have to risk your life. See that you share both one flesh and one humanity.

42 "Gather around you those who are feet and hands of the people; do not greet them indifferently; do not carry with negligence your respective loads. For you are eagles, you are tigers, and you are the support and the remedy.

43 "If someone overcomes you, let him go ahead. You should not be first at the entrance. When there is speaking, do not be the first to talk. If Ometeotl is not giving you a signal, do not take the lead. If you are given that which you need at the end, do not be mad. And if you are given nothing, be grateful anyway. Heaven wanted it that way. It is deserved.

44 "Do not wish to have your food in a hurry; instead, be moderate, austere, and see that others eat first. Then take some water and wash their hands and mouths. Not because they are nobles will you lose your own nobility, nor will your jades or turquoises fall from your busy hands.

45 "In any place you will find the one who works, the one who expresses himself, the one who reflects, the one who creates. Then do not be a nuisance there, do not cause problems there because of your ignorance.

46 "Be aware! In any place you can unconsciously break a head, transgress against someone, urinate on someone, make someone lose his good word, or ignore a good piece of advice.

47 "Treat with humanity those who surround you. You might find them anywhere: an old man, an old woman, a sick person, or a child. Therefore, you have no excuse.

48 "Do not allow your heart to be your father and mother. Do not allow the scattered ashes and the crossroads to give you orders. Do not let your desire devour your foot. Do not allow a skirt to move you ardently. All these spoils wear out and soil a man.

49 "Do not allow your strength to make you arrogant. Do not let your understanding be your support. Do not brag about your convictions. Do not build your house on your own opinions. You are only a little bird, a jade bead . . . barely a feather.

50 "Do not go into someone else's coffer. Do not support yourself from someone else's plate. Do not invite yourself to the banquet. Do not allow your destiny to depend on chance. All these are dangerous; they tie you and bind you.

51 "Do not act without reflecting or deliver yourself without caution. Do not begin work without planning or impose yourself without serene consideration. Do not accept what you don't deserve or abuse what you haven't created and what is not your prerogative. Do not let yourself be the object of begging and do not always expect to be offered things. Do not be warned twice because you have a heart inside you. Do not claim what is not yours.

52 "At planting time, do not merely go and plant; prepare yourself, be centered, be selective, plant well, sprout healthy roots. Cultivate your land, your fields, and your *nopales*.[9] Build a good and solid house there with everyone's help and leave it as inheritance to those that you are educating." So he told them.

53 Various people had come to hear Ce Acatl's words. Someone asked him: "Teacher, what kind of ritual would you advise so that we can be heard by the gods?" He answered them: "Ask in full humility and plead with justice. This is the synthesis of the whole ritual. For the lip that manifests itself pleading offers compensation and gives out satisfaction."

54 Then someone else said: "Teacher, I would like to know how the gods move about in heaven. Which is the way they take to come down to earth?" He answered him: "Could it be that you already know everything about walking on earth? Aren't you only just now testing the ground with your feet? Are you yet leading yourself? Aren't you still taken and carried? Will we get to know all this tomorrow or after tomorrow? Perhaps only he, the master of intimate closeness, knows it."

55 A wealthy merchant had come closer to listen. He then asked: "What can you say to us, the ones who carry the load of the people?" Ce Acatl answered him: "One must receive inheritance and fortune with worry and sorrow. Warm is the house and the home of the poor, and his wife and children are tranquil.

56 "Be honest. Pay your tribute. Do not be afraid of hard work. Love those who are your sustenance. Plead to them, do not go against them. Have only gestures of reverence and acquiescence for them. Even more, help them and support their hands and feet, for the work they give you as a service is great."

57 Another listener told him: "The idea of leaving my father and mother to follow you and your companions is tormenting me."

58 He answered him: "Concentrate only on Ometeotl. The name of the one capable of everything is the only cause for joy. He shares his glory over there, on the heights, for everyone. And when a good man receives it he becomes like an excellent bird: From his tail and wings, fathers and mothers come out, those who are guiding us in any place of the universe in which we exist.

59 "You could be living by his side right at this moment, on this day that you have come to borrow from him. Go back to his side and be conscious of your owner. When you neglect him, he is hurt and annoyed, and because you both are one, his sorrow and abandonment returns to your heart.

60 "Even more, enjoy the wealth of the one who torments you, the one who makes you pure. For he has placed in you his water of an intense blue, his water of jades, and his cup of turquoise to wash your soul and your life so you will deserve your own existence."

61 A young man from the nobility asked him: "Is my birth a product of chance, or something that I deserved? Ce Acatl then asked the young one: "Were you born a noble? Beware of that. It could intoxicate you or make you arrogant. Have you reached nobility? Here is what makes you a noble: the creation of a lineage. The taking of a torch and soap, chili and lime, plough and seeds. Work and be of service. Truly, this is what makes us noble.

62 "They say there is an heir to the throne. This is how he should show his standing: He must lower his head and salute with humility. He must show special consideration to the eagle and to the tiger. To the deserving one[10] he must show respect for his humble girdle and poor clothes. If in his way he finds an old woman or an old man, he must say: 'My father, my grandmother, let peace be your guide so that your feet will not stumble.'"

63 A young Cholutec came near and said to him: "In order to be a Toltec, I have tried to follow your teachings, but when I see the pain and the human misery, my heart hesitates." He then answered: "Do not be sad for human pain and misery; do not be sick or tormented because of it. Do not lose weight over it. Is it that only compassion and blandness should be our faith? Be a warrior.

64 "Do not allow your fear to faint before crookedness, before duplicity, the thing that divides us. Instead, throw yourself onto him, the being from heaven, the one who gives us life. Attach yourself with all your strength to an elevated vision and go with him; throw yourself onto him. It will happen that he will become the roots of your self.

65 "Concentrate on him wherever you are; keep him close to your face, to your heart. Find and acknowledge what is asked of you on this earth. Go about this in a way that is similar to looking for something with only the touch of your hands: step by step as when you are painting a book.

66 "Find out what misfortune consists of so that you will not live in that way, with unhappiness, inhumanity, the loss of something. Walk only in your own peace and your own prudence, without resting, without doubts. For in that way you will not sadden my heart. Live serenely, with all your attention."

67 Somebody from the group praised him with these words: "Teacher, you have become like a willow, like a staff; that is the reason I have come to be counted, to rest by your side. You are ceiba and willow, you are balm and remedy. In your hands I will grow green again and I will be renewed, for you have washed me, you have cleansed me, you have made me pure. Only until now, having made you my father and mother, do I find rest and healing. I have come to be healed by you; I have come to be healed at your side. I am grateful to you."

68 He answered him: "Now that Ometeotl has shown you his goodness, now that he is moving in your inner being, now that he inside you is panting, do not forsake him. Do not play with your inner conviction so that later on, disgusted, you will give it back to him wondering, 'Have I truly been healed?' No, don't go about it that way. Now that you have come closer to the wealth that his presence brings, will you offend him again? Will you soil your being and your soul again?

69 "If you fall many times, after all, if you again remember your god and sincerely cleanse yourself before him and rid yourself of your stain in his presence, once again he will have pity on you and his eyes will look at you. So enjoy your treasure, for it comes from our God's bosom."

70 Somebody there had difficulty speaking to his own heart, for his mind was wandering and his heart was not still. Ce Acatl sat by his side and said: "Come and enter into Ometeotl's bliss. Lower your head, strengthen your knees, take on an attentive posture and allow your legs to become used to it. Flow gently toward our lord. Is something tormenting you? Is something interfering with your flow? Scatter it in his joy and you will strengthen your life."

71 All night long they talked about diverse matters. Finally, he told them: "This that I am feeding you is pure nourishment. Understand that which is to be eaten here in these lands. Take it closer to your faces at once. Do not become like stones, for you already know that if a stone is hard, you will strike it more than once before it breaks.

72 "See: When they chase him, the deer is scared; he has no idea that he is going to the void, to death. And you? By any chance are you a deer who doesn't know where he is going? The way has been shown to you. If you lose the way, you will betray your own will.

73 "See how the flowery tree does not grow green again, does not sprout again. It only comes to life if it is able to withstand the frost, otherwise it withers and dries up. If you don't grow green again and sprout branches in the right season of your will, you will throw yourselves into the mouths of beasts."

74 In this way his followers learned and became Toltecs. They became very precise in divine matters. They only had one god whom they invoked and pleaded to: Quetzalcoatl. Every thing Ce Acatl told them to do, they did without disappointing him and without any omissions. His disciples became believers and that is how they became wise and rich in love, and they were happy.

> 🌀 Sources for this chapter: *Códice Florentino* and *Huehuetlahtolli de Padre Olmos*.

1. Thy bodies and thy souls. This text can be taken as the creed of Quetzalcoatl's religion.
2. According to this theology, God's existence is completed in humanity.
3. Thirteen is a key number in the construction of the solar system and the unfolding of the sacred seven.
4. The Nahua moon cycle consisted of only twenty days.
5. The ideal human age was computed in a *huehuete,* meaning 104 years.
6. This means a person who both receives and reflects.
7. With talk and gossip.
8. Hallucinogen.
9. An edible cactus abundant in Mexico.
10. This refers to Macehual, the one who deserves through sacrifice to the gods; the humble one. Eagle and tiger are two ranks of common soldier.

CHAPTER TWELVE
THE BANQUET

1 On a given day, the most important people of the country gathered in the city. They had been summoned to a grand banquet. To make a big show of a piety that he did not feel, the king of Cholula also asked Ce Acatl to attend the feast. Therefore, he sent messengers with the invitation.

2 Ce Acatl came to the palace wearing his robe of penitence and asked to be taken to the banquet room. The door guards were warned that a poor beggar wanted to see the king, but the king ordered the beggar to be thrown out on the street.

3 After some hours, seeing that the prince of Tula wasn't coming, the king sent another messenger to convince Ce Acatl to attend the banquet. Then Ce Acatl wrapped his royal dress and his priestly insignias and sent the bundle with the messenger.

4 This enraged the king of Cholula. For the third time he sent a messenger to Ce Acatl's dwelling with the entreaty: "I beg you to come to the banquet in person, for it is proper for the business of state." With this, the penitent went to the palace.

5 There were many guests in the banquet hall. Silence fell when they saw Ce Acatl. He then took the floor and said: "Today we are favored by the divine being, the prodigious one, the beginning of all existence, the perfect serenity, the one for whom we all live. Today he makes us his captives; his heart binds us. Should we be silent?"

6 "You, Cholutec: Do you feel hard and strong? Are you, perhaps, made of wood or of stone? When our God grows tired of you, when he becomes bored and forgets about you, will you hide in a hollow? Or will you climb a tree? Or perhaps you will hide beneath the water, or run away to the mountains and find refuge in a cave.

7 "Did you find me ugly without my adornments? We all are like that: dust, pure mud. Whatever adorns us is nothing but appearance. When our time comes for walking in the land of the mystery, what will our remains be like? What will our skulls look like?

8 "Oh king! Ometeotl is governing us in the way he understands. Assume your rise and fall wherever you go, your appearance and essence, your ugliness and adornments, for you are nobody. Go to God's lap, where truly we become somebody, where truly we grow. Perhaps he will be moved to warn you when he grows tired. Perhaps he will allow you to place yourself at his feet.

9 "Do not focus on feathers and jade, for these will perish. Look instead upon what surpasses us; look inside heaven. There is the treasure Ometeotl, the true man, the friend, the loved one, the one who gives, decides, takes, and makes us grow.

10 "You who is carried in a litter, listen well: Do not forget what is dear, what can fulfill you, what you need, what I give to you today. Take advantage of what he places by your side. See to it that it engages you, that it lifts you up. I encourage you to receive it!"

11 On hearing these words, the king of Cholula felt ashamed and, prostrating himself, he made a public confession: "Divine representative, here your presence has shaken me to the core and before you I want to expose my filth and faults. For I have stolen and lied, I have committed adultery, and I have despised children.

12 "Lord, give me relief, give me remedy; for I am walking alone and am falling from the precipice. I feel as though hail is falling on me and the wind is whipping me. To whom should I commend myself?" And he showed Ce Acatl great adoration in front of his guests.

13 From then on, the king of Cholula became a very good friend of Ce Acatl and his followers, attending to their needs and giving them his favor. Even more, he saw to it that the great temple was rejuvenated, and he created retreats for Quetzalcoatl's priests whom he attracted to the city from all corners of the kingdom. Time and again he asked to be accepted into the community of monks, but Ce Acatl, in the interest of the people of the city, did not concede to him.

Sources for this chapter: *Leyenda del Tepozteco; Códice Florentino;* and *Huehuetlahtolli de Padre Olmos.*

CHAPTER THIRTEEN

THE PRIESTS OF THE GOD OF DEATH

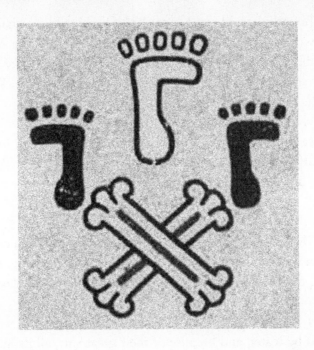

1 It so happened that there came to Cholula certain partisans of Tezcatlipoca who were preaching new ideas about the destiny of human bodies and souls after death. In opposition to them were some priests of the god of death whose salaries depended on performing funeral traditions. A great discussion was unleashed between them and they could not come to an understanding.

2 They went then to the disciples of Ce Acatl to ask that they be arbiters of their discussion, but the disciples were not able to do so. They then decided to look for their teacher.

3 They found the penitent meditating on the ball-game field, and there they asked him: "Teacher, what are your teachings regarding human death, the destiny of the body and the soul, and the nature of funeral rites?" He responded: "Before I answer you I would like to hear your explanations."

4 The Tezcatlipoca adepts began: "The body is like a chalice filled with flowers, while the soul is like the blossoms' perfume. When the flowers die, the body and soul die as well. The body is like a page in a book without paint; the soul is an illuminated figure. When the book falls into the fire, everything disappears.

5 "There is only one way to escape our human destiny: by becoming an offering from a pure heart, by going ahead of death and mocking her with your sacrifice. Only in this way can we come to be gods."

6 Then the priests of the god of death took the floor and explained: "There are many ways of living and many ways of dying, therefore there are many types of bodies and of souls, and many destinies.

7 "This is what our elders have said: Long ago, the world was destroyed by water, and because of their great sins, all its inhabitants perished by drowning. They descended to the inferno where they were burned in its flames. We, the ones who have come after, should burn our people's bodies after death and keep the ashes, for in this way the lord of the dead will allow us to be born again in new bodies.

8 "The souls of sinners will be burned and will go to the grave and the snare, to the mouth of the reptile and to battle. They will move endlessly among tempestuous winds and needles of ice until they are cleansed of their faults.

9 "But the bodies of these will not be burned: those touched by lightning, those who have drowned, the lepers, those who are sick with chronic and contagious disease. They will be sent back to earth in their clothes and their souls will live in endless amusement with the sons of Tlaloc.

10 "And the bodies of the warriors, priests, ascetics, the sacrificed, painters, poets, princes, children, slaves who have died in the fields, and the women who have died in childbirth will not be burned. They will be buried with honors and their souls will go to the fields of the sun where they will be accompanied forever by flowers and chanting.

11 "After four years, their souls will return as butterflies and birds to flutter about for a time before going back to Ometeotl, from whom we all parted. This is what we know."

12 Then Ce Acatl answered them: "By chance, have you heard the elders speaking in this way when they dispose of the dead? Is he already God? And perhaps you have heard this song: Lord, wake up, wake up, the day is breaking, the golden birds begin their singing, the butterflies are already flying.

13 "Do not deceive yourselves. The dead ones do not die; they wake up. We who live here are not really living; we are dreaming. To die is to become a god, a sun, a moon, a star, the wind, the sea, the land. Understand this: The dead ones wake up from this life's dream. Be they wise men, nobles, or slaves, they all go to the land of mystery.

14 "Consider this and take advantage of it: We do not live twice and we do not die twice. Our life is unique. Whether you are good or bad, your actions were like good or bad paint, a color that vanishes with time and forgetfulness."

Sources for this chapter: *Historia general de las cosas de la Nueva España* and *Cantares de los señores de la Nueva España*.

CHAPTER FOURTEEN
THE DREAM

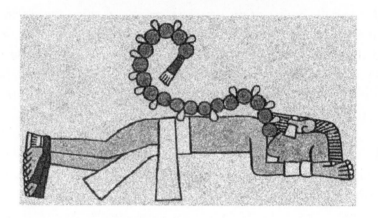

1 Year Thirteen Tochtli (998 C.E.). One night Ce Acatl had a dream in which appeared a necklace of unmatchable beauty, made with golden grains of maize. The necklace was spinning in space by itself, then it broke apart and its grains were scattered all over. The penitent became frightened and screamed, and the sound of his own voice awoke him. He stood up on his mat, called his followers to come closer, and said to them:

2 "Listen, my friends, to the dream of one word! Each spring the golden corncob revives us. The red corncob opens our eyes. The necklace from its grains comforts and illuminates us. See: The necklace is breaking, its grains are scattering." With this he announced his coming transformation.

3 Then he added: "Spring is coming to an end, summertime is arriving. The sun inflames the battle, the rains are beginning. Men must be dragged down, the country must be ruined. It is time, my friends, for the ice to break, for the clouds to completely cover the sun and moon across the world. It is time for the torrents of dissolution to fall and end the memory of all suffering.

4 "It is time to sweep and gather and throw away the dust. It is time to tear up the tunic and trample it underfoot. It is time to get rid of the mask that is keeping us under cover. Who is going to protect you then, orphans of mother, orphans of father? To whom will you go for shelter?" So he told them.

5 When they realized that he was telling them of his departure, the apprentices became sad. They said: "Is it not so that here with the Cholutecs we are better off than ever?" Timal asked Ce Acatl: "When will we see all this?"

6 He answered: "When the sun and the moon join. When night and the day come at the same time. When you sink deep into the abyss and the new day finds you there. When the numbers nine and thirteen unite. When you see movement above and movement below and the serpent of light and life without end is born. Yet on this earth you will see all this and the will of the one will come to be. See: The consecration of a new life is already descending from the heart of heaven."

7 After speaking, he asked them to put all their business in order, and to be ready for their departure.

Sources for this chapter: *Cantares de los señores de la Nueva España* and *Chilam Balam, libro de los libros*.

CHAPTER FIFTEEN
THE EMBASSY

1 When the Cholutecs learned about the penitent's desire to continue on his way, they sent an embassy made up of the foremost priests to dissuade him. But he did not want to hear their reasons and told them:

2 "The time has come, my friends. See: I only have one life and it is suffering. My own people chased, stalked, and tricked me, but you offered me shelter. My heart has been destined for sacrifice, and you, for a short while, have made me happy.

3 "The time has come to an end. I have chosen to march forward. Friends, do not stop me, do not increase my pain. I am going to the house of mystery, to the precious scale.[1] I am going to the edge of the divine water where the green jade is.

4 "The mother calls, the son has descended. It is time to go back. Rejoice and come with me. Come forward you, the ones with oppressed hearts. Open with me the coffer of your souls, spill the flowery wine of your lives. Do not fear, my friends, it is the springtime of the one for whom we all live. Very soon his chanting will adorn this temple. Listen!"

5 But the Cholutecs did not want to hear him. One of them took his hand and told him: "Because of your skills and knowledge you have come here. Precious twin, you who makes things shine. Think now and take pity on yourself. Remember how our grandfathers also went to the house of mystery, and there they sank. We inherited only their absence. In vain you start this war. Oh, you who meditates! The one for whom we all live has unhinged your judgment.

6 "You broke the jades, the bracelets. You tore the broad plumage. There was a shower of weeping in your house. And yet you are disposed to you yourself being destroyed? Perhaps your heart will perish as well?

7 The priest answered Ce Acatl with these words of complaint, for in Cholula they loved him greatly and didn't want to lose him. But Ce Acatl interrupted this speech and told him: "What is this that you say, grandfather? Have you really had me among you? Have you truly had need of me? Think about your words, priest. You have no one. We are forever alone on earth.

8 "Do not suffer. I know pain. With anguish we live on the earth. All Ometeotl's rage has poured this way. But ask your memory: Is this our true house? Observe the signals: Our existence is found in another place."

9 He then requested of those surrounding him: "Do not ponder, friends, or think about our death. Do not deceive yourselves. By our side the beautiful flowers are sprouting, the ones that are the joy of the one for whom we all live. We all remember past moments, and that makes us sad. But think about it: All heroes were formed in the same way, with pain and anguish. Do not cry on account of departed princes. No one will remain here forever."

Source for this chapter: *Cantares de los señores de la Nueva España.*

1. The Toltecs believed that heaven was a scale of thirteen levels.

CHAPTER SIXTEEN

"I GREET YOU"

1 Determined as he was, Ce Acatl wanted to say goodbye to the people of Cholula. Ten years he lived with them, and he had received nothing but affection at all times. Therefore, he sent his followers with messages of gratitude for the shared friendship. They went with the nobles and the poor and exchanged with all of them words of love and the promise of returning to see them.

2 Upon learning about the departure, the king of Cholula organized a farewell ceremony during which he spoke: "My lord, stand up, there where you have been for a moment, for a day, right next to the god of intimate vicinity, the owner of the house, the divine king and proprietor of the sandals that you are wearing and on whose left you are, the one you assist and represent. For you are his interpreter, you are the speaker and the witness of his word.

3 "You are eagle and tiger, you are your own gift and you are what you deserve; you are intrepid; you are a singer! The breath, the word of our God does not bloom in vain! He has entrusted it to your hands, he keeps the book and the paint, so red and so black, in your bosom and in your throat! And for an answer you throw us eagle darts and tiger arrows.

4 "Why did you go there, where the great mirror with two faces is, the one that at the break of day is in both the world of the dead and heaven. And there you saw the curve of the universe expand from the world of the dead to heaven, there where the thick torch is that neither expels smoke nor casts any shadows, the one that lights all the corners of the world, manifesting its own dawn, its sun, its water, its mountain.

5 "For he gave you hands, he gave you feet, he gave you a tail and wings that you spread so well. He gave you a people and a city that, under your guidance, long for him. For he painted you, he gave you colors and lips and teeth, he gave you distinction and glory. That is how he has strengthened you. He showed you his cloth, he dressed you in white, and adorned you with feathers. That is how he chose you and gave you power.

6 "Oh penitent, you honored his kingdom and made prosperous his dominion. For here among us, great was your effort. You did slave's work to lead us toward his mat and throne.

7 "Cholutecs! Here before you is the brave warrior, the one who has no rest during the daytime, who does not lie down. The one who endures tooth and nail, hunger and penitence, our exaltation and dejection, the trap, the snare, and the hole.

8 "Here before you is the one who defends jade, turquoise, and the broad, gleaming, and waving plume that is always green. He is the genuine eagle, the authentic tiger; the one who has come to preserve things and people and make them grow; the one who gives flowering and renewal; the one who shines and dignifies; the one who is worthy of veneration.

9 "Here we proclaim your light and shadow, your fall and your rebirth. We have seen your weeping, your sweat. We have seen your fatigued body, your suffering flesh. We see that you don't live in peace, that you don't rest in sleep. Your face is tired, your heart struggles in the waves. Fear surrounds you here, anxiety is at your back. You threw away your wealth; food and water are separated from your lips. Here we proclaim your exaltation and your dejection.

10 "Only in this way, with your hands on your heart, with extreme difficulty and great penitence, did you achieve the power, the kingdom. Only in this way have you come to be a true relief for the people and a counselor to the throne.

11 "Today your pleasure is great, your responsibility is wide. You are ceiba and willow, roof and shelter, guide, rest, and balm. Within you and by your side we shelter ourselves, we your subjects, your blood and color, your shoots and renewal, the ones who follow in your footsteps and look to your guidance, the ones who are willing and of a noble race.

12 "Oh leader of men, strength of people! You of the broad back and sure steps. You have become a garden of fruit. You elevate yourself with sweetness, you bloom with grace. Birds of many colors find relief by your side; they are protected from the sun in your hands.

13 "The bowl of jade is in your hands by the green waters and by the blue waters where the dew-covered reed rises, the one you rattle and shake over the birds. That is how you wash them; that is how you clean them. And the thick brush and broad comb are in your hands, the scorpion and nettle as well, the frozen water and the whipping staff. That is how you reprimanded us.

14 "In your hands are the drill, the fine sand, and the dense brush—the ones with which you sand, smooth, and polish. You choose and match the slender jade, well lined and better drilled; the broad turquoise, well polished and well rounded. You arrange the necklace and the garland of feathers. You select everything that is of value, place it in its proper place, and keep it sheltered. This you offer freely.

15 "For you paint and give color to the writing in the book; you choose the ink, the design, the size. You are a sculptor and you define the lines. Your name will never be forgotten. Your fame will never be erased. I greet you, oh priest!

16 "Perhaps the dual princes passed over you to give you their guidance and their condition? Did you fulfill the ancient promises? Did the signals that we were waiting for turn to flesh in you, so that we might have you as a prince and as a god? I greet you, oh penitent!

17 "Now Ometeotl has called you and it is time for farewell and weeping. Do not allow your people to remain behind! Wherever you go, guide us on your good path. I will ensure that you don't become sick or infected. I will not allow any plagues to take you. Go in peace, divine messenger, and allow your apprentices to go with you. Try, oh my lord!"

    Source for this chapter: *Huehuetlahtolli de Padre Olmos.*

CHAPTER SEVENTEEN

THE RELICS

1 When Ce Acatl was leaving the city, the Chulula elders sent a message to him saying: "Lord, given the fact that you are persuaded to go on toward the land inhabited by the sun, your father, and because we are afraid we might not ever see you again, we ask nothing of you but that you leave something for us to remember you by.

2 "By seeing you continuously in this way, we will never forget you or your commandments. By seeing your keepsake, our children will know that a divine lord was the recipient of our hospitality, and even our enemies will learn to respect us in the exercise of peace, if they have knowledge of your legacy."

3 Fearing that in having something to see and touch they would forget his words, he didn't consent. He did not want to leave a relic.

But the messengers were so persistent that he took pity on them and he forced himself to agree.

4 Ce Acatl saw to it that some green stones were worked in the image of birds and serpents, and one of them was made into a very good likeness of a monkey's head. Then he gave them the stones. They placed them, along with other revered and valued objects in the city, in a tiger-skin bag. And then they asked for a few hairs from his beard. These they greatly valued and, after that, called them the beard of the sun.

5 These objects remained in the great temple of Cholula. And the authority represented by them was such that from then on no enemy dared to war against the Cholutecs. Each year, pilgrims and people from all corners of the world would gather at the sanctuary where these relics were kept.

 Source for this chapter: *Historia de las indias.*

PART FOUR

Let the earth remain!
Let the mountains stand!
Let the perfumed cacao flowers
be scattered across the world!
Let the earth remain!

CHAPTER ONE

INVOCATION TO MOTHER EARTH

1 When Ce Acatl set out from Cholula, many loyal followers went with him. They loved the penitent so much that they abandoned their possessions and trusted him with their women, their children, and their infirm. They all stood up and began the march, even the old women and the old men; all of them wanted to accompany him. All were set in motion.

2 They arrived at the first campground toward nightfall. He gathered them and invoked the protection of heaven and earth.

3 "Oh, deities of the elements, Ometeotl, unique being, lady of the earth, protective mother! Take heed of the uncertainties of our way and come to our aid. We beg this of you.

4 "Let not any kind of pain offend us on our way—black, brown, or green pains.¹ If the divine ones from the jungle attack us, those who run on their hands and feet, come in our favor, precious Lord. See that I, the penitent, am asking you, Quetzalcoatl.

5 "And you, Lord Nanahuatzin, sun and light that guides us, help us to go ahead of you, to walk first as you follow so that before you finish your divine walk we have already passed through valleys and ravines, over ridges and mountains. In this way your glory will not burn us.

6 "Don't allow the ground's roughness to harm us or the face of the earth to devour us. Let us walk with you in the center of heaven, for in this way our feet will not stumble and our souls will not be frightened.

7 "Send us, Lord, your four hundred children to protect us. See that we have no blood or color, for we are ascetics. Come, take us over the mountain and take us through the ravine. Come singing. Who has created it? Who has forged it? Not me.

8 "Come, with your leaves as wings, creature of dampness, for it is time to walk, time to lead those with spiritual faces and hearts, the ones who are hungry and thirsty for your cause, oh Lord.

9 "And you, Mother Earth, divine lady upon whose face we carelessly tread, do not lash out at us in anger, do not harm us. Oh Mother Earth, be like the she-rabbit that lies down and sleeps; let us gently knead your innumerable breasts. Turn over onto your back."

10 In this way, favored with the invocation, the pilgrims readied themselves for marching in the direction of the sunrise, to the interior of the sea and the land of red and black, the land of glory and wisdom. Because the pilgrims were vast in number, they traveled slowly around the mountains. They stopped frequently in different places, sharing with the inhabitants of those lands, giving them the news of the penitent's teachings, and inviting them to join their group.

11 As they journeyed, they passed villages, mountains, rivers, springs, and ravines. Ce Acatl changed the traditional names of these places, giving them new ones with suitable meanings. These are the names they have today.

Sources for this chapter: *Tratado de las idolatrías* and *Historia de las indias.*

1. For the Toltec people, illness and pains were spirits of the mountains, hence their colors.

CHAPTER TWO
THE BOOK

1 On passing through a small city called Ocuituco, Ce Acatl was received by its inhabitants with songs and tears. Realizing that their hearts were in distress, for they all sensed his coming banishment, he addressed them: "Cheer up, my true friends! Only for an instant and only for one mandate was our love born. Remember this and your tribulations will cease."

2 Because they also asked him for a legacy, he gave them a book with all his words, advice, songs, and deeds. To this day this large book, about four fingers thick, remains with the elders of Ocuituco.

3 The rest of his deeds—his arrival at the divine water, the bonfire, his ascent as a bright star that accompanies the sun, all of it—is registered in a separate commentary.

Sources for this chapter: *Historia de las indias* and *Códice Chimalpopoca.*

CHAPTER THREE

THE BRIDGE

1 Following their route, they came to a place were the land broke and came down to a deep, low-lying area. There a wide river flowed. The pages looked for a way to cross it but could not find one. They tried many times, but just as many times they retreated, frightened, for the waves crashed, making a great roar. Sitting in the shade of some large rocks, Ce Acatl observed their efforts.

2 On seeing that there was no way to pass and that the current was rushing beyond measurement, the pages began lamenting for their lives. Their lack of heart annoyed the penitent and, coming closer, he reprimanded them.

3 "Cowards! What are you afraid of? Who knows if we must live or we must die? How can you determine from here what is recorded? Tomorrow or after tomorrow, won't we all depart? Why do you hesitate, precipitating the end in this way? Make an effort! We will come to know the mystery."

4 There at the edge of the river was a mound of stones. Ce Acatl, feeling that the spirit of Ometeotl penetrated his body, struck a stone with his foot while at the same time pronouncing in a great voice. The stone broke apart and fell in the water, creating a bridge over which they could pass. The bridge can still be seen in that place. It is called Ripped Stone.[1]

Sources for this chapter: *Historia general de las cosas de la Nueva España; Historia de las indias;* and *Cantares de los señores de la Nueva España.*

1. In physiological context this break represents the cardiac center in which powerful currents of energy converge. An inadequate attempt to cross the torrent might destroy the human soul.

CHAPTER FOUR

THE THINKERS

1 They came to another place where a group of anchorites were dwelling in solitude. Having forgotten the world, they fed themselves only from their deep thoughts. Two of them were sunbathing on the trunk of a fallen tree.

2 On seeing them, Ce Acatl stepped forward to greet them and asked: "Grandfathers, what are you doing here? What are you looking for in this solitude, separated from life like expressionless corpses while others come and go?"

3 The eldest of the ascetics opened his mouth and told him: "Lord, we are looking for the power of the thirteen, the beautiful flower! Come with us!"

4 He answered: "Grandfathers, no one as precious as the eagle that flies has been made by the one for whom we all live, no one as

perfect as the tiger, heart of the mountain. And even they are sub-
missive to the duty of his works!"

5 The ascetic observed: "My son, even the eagle must cease her
screaming and the tiger will give up his colors. There in the house of
mystery, where no one is expecting us, will someone differentiate
our faces? Acknowledge our works? Keep an account of our aspira-
tions?"

6 He continued: "Look, pilgrim, those who come and go quickly
tire. Beauty withers and pleasure spends itself. If it is true that we
have come to feed death, then we can wait for her in this way:
motionless and in silence. That is the reason we are here."[1]

7 Ce Acatl started to retreat. But the spirit of Tezcatlipoca entered
into the ascetics and moved them to tempt him with questions. They
asked him: "Pilgrim, can you tell us who you are, where you are
coming from, and where you are going? Can you, in all truth, tell us
what you are looking for?"

8 He answered: "Old ones, I am the lone one. I have come and I
have gone. It is for you to consider whether or not this was easy for
me, you who remain on the fringes of men. My heart was broken
just as jade was broken, and I still exist. I must extinguish myself,
old ones, that is the order of the One. I go where the waters swell to
deliver myself."

9 Ce Acatl said further: "Could it be that you know what I'm talking about? Could it be that you know why people perish? How does
man become an orphan here? Do you remember the banner of gold
and the light of the house of dawn? I, the sinner, the penitent, am
going there.

10 "For a brief time the one for whom I exist hides from me, and
I can hardly bear it. How can I wait calmly when I am going back
home?" So Ce Acatl spoke.

11 After looking at them with sadness for a moment, he added, "Your work is useless and your anguish is in vain, looking for your place through such austerity. Oh reflective ones, embittered ones! How can you be quiet when you are at a feast?

12 "We have life once and only once. One day we appear, and the next night we are no longer here. Come to rest in my friendship, you who are weary of the world! Heal your pain here!" So he told them.

13 The ascetics did not respond. They stood there in silence, absorbed in their thoughts, with their petrified faces and their bodies as quiet as funerary bundles. Seeing no sign that they had heard his words, Ce Acatl went back to his people and departed from there.

 Source for this chapter: *Cantares de los señores de la Nueva España.*

1. These ascetics lived isolated in the mountains. Some of them were dedicated to fakirlike practices, such as contemplating the sun the whole day, never bathing, or engaging in very intense physical exercises. They were adepts to Tezcatlipoca.

CHAPTER FIVE

BY THE TREE

1 Ce Acatl arrived at another place, which, back then, was called By the Tree. There was on that spot an old *sabino,* quite corpulent and very tall, with shade that extended over the land. Many birds were sheltered there.

2 Ce Acatl stopped for a moment under the tree and rested against its trunk. His body felt bruised and defeated. As he looked at his hands, he became somber and said: "Truly, I am old!" Then he ran away from there. From that time on that place was known as Old Tree.[1]

3 Later he thought: "This tree has seen too much. I must cut him down." He then acquired a copper ax, came to the sabino, and said to the tree:

4 "Put yourself in my place, you, nine times a stroked one, son of our own mother, the one of the skirt of stars; you who go down to the inferno and up to heaven. You are a lord of both worlds—put yourself in my place and ask, "Am I, perhaps, food for you?"[2] Don't you see that I am a penitent, a thin and bruised pilgrim without direction? Don't you have pity?

5 "Now, cheer up! It is I, the priest Quetzalcoatl, prince of the Nahuales, the Toltec. And I bring with me the one you see as a demon, rude and sharp, the one that shines as a red mirror.[3] For you have fancied me, for you almost took me, you that delights in the waters.

6 "Now, what are you thinking about? The moment has come for you to throw your thorns to the left, to the kingdom of that savage red demon that you so fear."

7 Ce Acatl then wounded the tree. With one stroke from the ax, he broke into the tree's body. He then took stones and threw them into the wound; he bombarded the trunk with stones, nicking it from top to bottom. And the stones that struck the tree encrusted it and there remained glued. This gash can be seen today, beginning at the base of the tree and going up to its crown. The tree is the Wounded Tree, the Tree of Old Age.[4]

🏵 Sources for this chapter: *Historia general de las cosas de la Nueva España; Historia de las indias;* and *Tratado de las idolatrías.*

1. The tree is a Nahual, Tezcatlipoca's twin, and wants to take over the vital force of the penitent.
2. Here Ce Acatl refers to the tree as an archetype of the vegetation that is destined to be harvested for use.
3. Here Ce Acatl is referring to the ax.
4. In esotericism, the tree represents heaven, the original place of human souls; it represents the axis of the world or the space-time dimensions. It also represents the human spinal column, with the stones in the trunk representing certain nerve nodules.

CHAPTER SIX

THE MUSICIANS OF THE SUN

1 Following Ce Acatl on his path were some contortionist dancers, their bodies all shaven and painted in yellow, wearing jangling anklets, holding rattles, and dancing. They placed themselves right in front of the pilgrims as they jumped and twisted and shouted, making a thousand graceful and grotesque gestures, like insects.[1]

2 The pilgrims watched the dancers with pleasure, for their movements were crazy and their words laughable. Some fell like old men and others pretended to be stupid or drunk. They spun themselves around, full of frenzy, or remained motionless for a long time in the strangest postures, or personified the wind and the gods, or fell to the ground and stood on their heads. They completely followed the law of their hearts.

3 When the penitent saw the dancers he was left full of admiration, so he asked them: "From where do you get your joy, friends? What manners are those in the land of god?"

4 One of them, the leader, answered him: "The giver of life has made us crazy; he has made us drunk! Those who have managed to find him are the ones who truly know love."

5 Ce Acatl greatly admired them after this answer, and he wanted to find out about the origins of these manners and this drunkenness. The dancer responded to him:

6 "Perhaps you do not know what Tezcatlipoca told my lord? 'Ehecatl,' he said, 'go across the sea to the house of the sun, where his musicians and singers praise him. Bring them back to earth with you, along with their instruments, so that they can serve men and rejoice and worship.'[2]

7 "Tezcatlipoca also ordered Ehecatl: 'Tell my servants to bind themselves to each other along the coast in order to form a bridge over which you can walk to the sun.'[3] Ehecatl did as he was told, and as he approached, the sun told his people: 'Look at the pitiful one! No one must answer his call. The one who does will have to accompany him.'

8 "When Ehecatl arrived at the sun, he began to shout, singing and jumping with joy. Nobody would answer him. But then one of the musicians from the sun heard his voice and, swept up by Ehecatl's joy, answered him. He was forced to descend to earth with Ehecatl. This musician is the one who, upon arriving on earth, gave us the dance and happiness with which your servants now rejoice."

9 The dancer finished his tale. Ce Acatl's spirit was transported by joy after listening to it. Then, unleashing his feet and his tongue, he too entered into the dance with the contortionists. His voice rose up and he sang:

10 "You, the one who dwells in the infinity of heaven! You, the one holding the city! You, the one who has the world in his hand like a jade bead! You, precious one among all that is precious, our father! All that exists does so because of you. Because of you, we bloom on earth like fruit. How great is the wealth of your flowers and your garlands! How, how can we obtain them?

11 "Now I know why I have always been waiting for you. I have been searching for your glory; I have pronounced your name. To be where you are, to sit by your side on your royal matting, to rejoice in your happiness is all I wish for, oh father. There where the shells are making eternal music, where the trumpets are resounding and the drum vibrates, where in their joy the sun dancers are dancing, only there I want to go, with you, my mother, my father!"

Sources for this chapter: *Memoriales; Códice Florentino;* and *Romances de los señores de la Nueva España.*

1. Contortionist dancers and their dances have existed elsewhere throughout history. Examples include the Chaitanya of medieval India and the Taki Onkoi, or "dancing illness," which existed in Peru in the eighteenth century.
2. Ehecatl is an avatar, a manifestation of Quetzalcoatl preceding Ce Acatl. In this context the name means "breath" or "spirit." Apparently, Ehecatl left a sect of dancers whose "footprints" appear in Olmec art and in Teotihuacan culture.
3. This bridge has several meanings. Directly it is an exercise of solar energetic stringing. In social terms, it is an image of the popular conception of the Messiah. In physiological terms, it alludes to the spiritual connection between the earth and the sun through the sea of the spiritual consciousness.

CHAPTER SEVEN

THE MOUNTAIN

1 Year One Acatl (999 B.C.E.). On nearing the sea, Ce Acatl and his followers, numbering about eight thousand people, settled themselves on a plain. The sea was located close to a very tall mountain called Mirror of the White and the Black, which extended both southward and northward from the edge of the water.[1]

2 Ce Acatl retired to this mountain to fulfill his tradition. On the way he stopped on a rock and arranged his instruments of penitence. The thorns afflicted his flesh, and he adorned the stone with red flowers.[2] Above, the stars trembled. An eagle passed over, screaming. In the darkness a tiger answered her.

3 "I came to water the flowers, oh father," said Ce Acatl, "flowers of war in the battlefield. They are your flowers, the ones you favor! Do not hide, dweller of the intimate living. Allow me to find you! Even if I die, allow me as a quetzal to fly to the interior of heaven where you are. Maybe in this way we will come to be friends. Maybe I will achieve true life."

4 Toward dawn, he descended. His heart was jumping and his face was transformed. It was frightening to see his tired body and the bloody bag where he kept his thorns.[3]

5 The pages had kept vigil. One of them saw him coming, stepped forward to receive him, and said: "Lord, the edge of the water is right before us. A hard journey on the road remains. Bid goodbye to the crowd so they will disperse and you will not endanger the elders and the children that have come to accompany you. Talk to them; perhaps they will listen to you."

6 But he answered: "How can I chase away these loyal warriors now that the day of the eagles and the time of the tigers has come?"

7 Then, with his hand he pointed to the mountain and ordered: "Let the valleys rise and the mountains become humble!" On the spot the great mountain cracked in the middle, and there was an open pass like a plain, like a flattened ball-game field. With the rumble of the earthquake the crowd of followers woke up, and a great fear overwhelmed them all.[4]

> ❇️ Sources for this chapter: *Historia de las indias; Romances de los señores de la Nueva España;* and *Historia general de las cosas de la Nueva España.*

1. Today this mountain is called Orizaba Peak.
2. This refers to a blood offering. The Toltec penitence included piercing various parts of the body with thorns.
3. The purpose for the pain of this technique of penance was to provoke a hormonal and steroidal rush and, along with it, a new state of consciousness.
4. The breaking of the mountain is a metaphor for the ego's submission to the will. In physiological terms, the mountain in front of the water alludes to the frontal nervous center, focused in the pituitary gland.

CHAPTER EIGHT

THE FIREWOOD TEMPLE

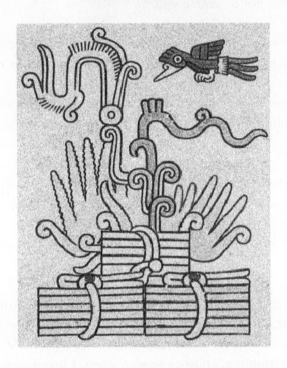

1 He then gave instruction for the building of a temple of logs over the mountain. For four days the pages carried the wood, to arrange it artfully into the shape of the temple. During this time, Ce Acatl kept to himself, fasting in solitude. Dark visions assaulted him, but his mother came to console him.

2 While he was fasting, within his heart he asked: "Before the altar of fire, my parents, I do not shame you! There where the gods reincarnated, where men became gods, I do not shame you. For my life on earth is finishing, and a new season and a New Kingdom are coming.

3 "Mother, woman, hear my prayer! You, dark lady, dweller of the rain's den, listen to my prayer. The flowery death has come down, she is already nearing me. In the world of red they invented her, the ancient ones, the ones who once were among us. The drink prepared long ago is moving closer to my mouth; I feel it. Mother, do not forsake me, I ask not to shame you."

4 While he was walking among the rocks, a roar like the sound of many trumpets, like the meeting of rushing waters, was heard, and before him his mother appeared, the Goddess of the Turquoise Skirt, wrapped in her dress of shining waves. The brilliance of the vision was blinding to the eye. Ce Acatl, not able to stand, fell down at her feet.

5 The goddess told him: "I, the Flowery Feather, Obsidian Butterfly, come from the region of the rain and darkness, from the house that is at the end, from the place of the origins. Are you calling me, priest of the spirit? Why are you lamenting? What is happening to you?"

6 He answered, "Lady, I have been given an appointment in the house of the sun, in the altar of fire, there where the gods were engendered. But see, my heart palpitates. I am like a mountain squirrel, scared, trembling, and I cling to a word. I love this life. That is the reason why my soul struggles and inside I am torn apart. Ah, you have given me such a hard task."

7 But the vision comforted him: "Cheer up, priest! Don't you see? Where the trumpets blare, there you must go. Do not fear pain, do not deceive yourself. The joy of divinity exists there alone. Leave the earth; go there! Perhaps in your heart you doubt? Oh penitent, perhaps you don't dare? If you truly love me, for everyone's benefit you must go to the region of the turquoise fog."[1]

Sources for this chapter: *Anales de Cuautitlán; Leyenda de los soles;* and *Romances de los señores de la Nueva España.*

1. In these words one can notice the doctrine of Macehualiztli, that of deserving, a redeeming pact between the gods and men.

CHAPTER NINE

THE BONFIRE

1 The moment had come. All the earth was delivered to the service of the house of god! Paper flags with butterflies of fire were raised everywhere. The men were standing, facing the four directions. Never before had such a sacrifice as this been prepared.

2 The face of the penitent was shining with the mark of God. But his friends were somber because, while readying the firewood temple, it became clear to them who was destined for the offering.

3 Observing their dejection, Ce Acatl gathered them around and told them: "Do not cry, my friends. I am a created being. I, the priest, should also stain myself with the dark red of blood."

4 Timal the warrior, driven by love, embraced Ce Acatl's knees and said to him: "Oh elder brother, prince of presages, sorcerer, you are leaving forever! That is why I cry. Now, send me with you to that mysterious place where you rule!"

5 But Ce Acatl made him rise and told him: "I came to rule mountains. Was it not written in your books long ago that I was to become a painter of souls, giver of life? Wake up, man, the sky is reddening, the sun is rising. The birds of fire are already singing; everywhere the sun's butterflies are stirring!"

6 He then gave the signal to his assistant. Quickly they dressed him with his royal insignias and dressed him with the green mask and the marvelous cloth embroidered with serpents. So arrayed, he walked toward the pyramid of timber.

7 As he ascended, he sang for himself: "In the temple of fire a man will be offered. Ah! A man must be offered. You go with sad lament to the land where somehow someone exists. You were celebrated, you pronounced divine words, but you are going to die. The one who is all compassion in truth demands this strange thing!"

8 On arriving at the sanctuary, he contemplated for the last time those who accompanied him. A deep silence reigned in the camp. It was the eighth house of the night, the house of masks. The sun was rising.

9 In his silence Ce Acatl heard his mother's voice urging him: "The night of ecstasy has come. Why do you reject it? The dawn of your triumph is rising. Sacrifice yourself now! Put on your dress of gold!"

10 He, acting alone, then set himself on fire. He raised his hands, lighting the whole temple at once, and he burned himself.

Sources for this chapter: *Anales de Cuautitlán* and *Romances de los señores de la Nueva España*.

CHAPTER TEN
THE ASCENDED HEART

1 When he burned, his ashes were lifted up on the spot. And all the beautiful birds that fly in the sky, those that were sent for his final hour, came to see them: golden birds, black birds, long-feathered birds with necks that stretched, birds that chanted beautifully and that flew serenely, and butterflies too. They all came.

2 Then there could be heard a great storm with rumbling thunder that spread over all the earth. A shadow hid the face of the sun, a rain of flowers whirled and fell. And the one for whom we all live came to hover over the land.

3 At that moment Ce Acatl's heart rose from the ashes, luminescent like a precious jade, and entered into heaven, escorted in the wind by the birds and butterflies.

4 The elders say that he became the morning star. They also say that this star only appeared after the death of the king, who, for this reason, is called Tlahuizcalpantecuhtli.[1]

Sources for this chapter: *Anales de Cuautitlán* and *Romances de los señores de la Nueva España.*

1. "The one who makes a dwelling from light."

CHAPTER ELEVEN

MATLAXOCHITL'S SONG

1 The fire burned for one day and one night. After that it became cold, and fog descended over the camp, darkening all colors. Lightning illuminated the sky with golden shields; there was feasting up there, but the earth was desolate.

2 Matlaxochitl cried for the penitent's death. In his pain he took the *teponaztle*[1] and sang: "In Tula there was a temple of fine wood. Its columns of feathered serpents are still standing there. He went away; our prince Naxcitl[2] has moved far away. We, his comrades, parted with him. Today we cry. In searching for the land of knowledge, we start from doom!

3 "We were there, in Cholula. Then we walked to Poyauhtecatitla, and we crossed the water at Acallan. Looking for the land of the wise men, we then turned east. Today we cry. We have departed toward ruin!

4 "I, the court's protector, wearing a beautiful headdress, have come to live among strangers. I am filled with tribulation, for my lord, the precious warrior, has gone away and has left me behind, orphaned. Oh, no!

5 "I cry because the mountains are crumbling. I lament because the sands of the sea have swirled. For my teacher has gone away, leaving me alone, orphaned.

6 "In the land of knowledge, there in the east, they were waiting for you. There they commanded your departure, and then you left. Oh my lord, precious warrior, you went away to rule over the celestial waters in the country of the morning bird.

7 "And here your houses, your bridge, your lordly mansion will remain. Here, completely abandoned, you leave behind the city of Tula, transformed from a place of upstarts. Look: The lord Timal and the nobles are crying endlessly.

8 "In Tula, where you governed as our prince, you are painted upon the stone and the wood, Naxcitl. Your name will never perish. Your favored ones will cry for you forever!

9 "You have built turquoise houses, serpents' houses, there in Tula where you ruled. You have left your chants for us. You gave an example. Oh, Naxcitl, your name will never be forgotten!"

Source for this chapter: *Códice Florentino.*

---

1. A teponaztle is an instrument consisting of a hollow wooden cylinder with two carved tongs to serve as keys. It is played with wooden mallets.
2. "Fourth step"; Ce Acatl's name in the order in the chain of Quetzalcoatl avatars.

CHAPTER TWELVE
THE ASHES

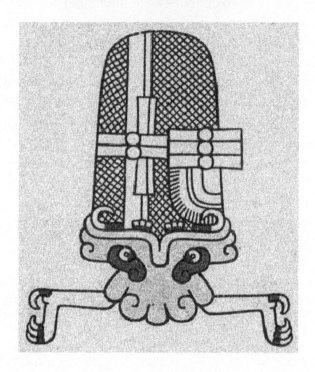

1 When the pages saw how sadly the people were contemplating the remains of the bonfire, they felt sympathy for them. So they gathered everyone around a stone, and when they were assembled, Macuilxochitl climbed to the top of it and spoke:

2 "Believe this, brothers, and do not torment yourselves: High in the temple, over his own shield, the one who descended transformed himself. He offered his heart in place of the honest word. It was him, the foreigner with the beaded necklace, truly it was him, the one we were waiting for, the feathered serpent!

3 "See: His breast opened like a flower and his heart ascended. He offered himself in a foreign country, in a strange land. With his royal staff and the sacred book he offered himself for us and for strangers, oh brothers!

4 "Our lord has departed. His body was broken. But his heart already flies toward the seven caverns, to the place of origin, there where the acacia is standing, where the eagle calls and the tiger roars, the place of his divine grandparents, the place that inspires veneration.

5 "Do not cry! He reached life. In the temple of fire he made war and won. He was born out of himself and became a son of gods. Thus we shall remember him forever.

6 "Firebird, wind of the sun, he flies in the middle of the great plains, toward the mystery. His heart has reached the heart of the heavens. Let his light be resplendent! Let happiness dwell in every good man!"

7 Then they gathered Ce Acatl's ashes and put them in bags of tiger skin so that they could be distributed all over the earth. The lords received these relics with great respect, and from that time they have revered them, to honor his memory.

Sources for this chapter: *Historia de las indias; Cantares de los señores de la Nueva España;* and *Relaciones históricas.*

CHAPTER THIRTEEN

IN THE REGION OF THE DEAD

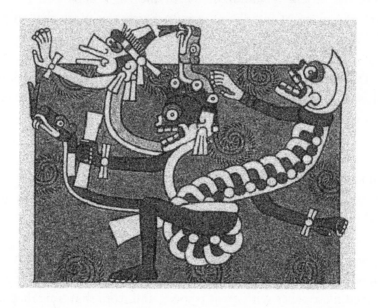

1 The old ones relate that after Ce Acatl died he was absent only four days. During that time he dwelled in the place of the dead where he talked with his ancestors. And this is what he did there:

2 Ce Acatl approached the place where the lord and the lady of the dead were sitting, and he greeted them: "Grandparents! I have come to seek out and take away the precious bones you are keeping; that is my mission and the reason I have been sacrificed."

3 The lord asked him: "What would you do with them, Quetzalcoatl?" And he answered: "The gods are preoccupied. There must be a new creation, a new word for the earth."

4 "So be it," the lord said. "If you sound the trumpet shell four times toward the four directions, and go around my precious circle four times, you will have them."[1]

5 But the lord gave him a shell without a hole; there was no way to make it sound. So Ce Acatl called the worms and told them: "Brothers, make me a hole through which I can breathe in and out." And so they did.

6 But he still could not make the shell sound, for he had no breath because he was dead. He then called to the bees and the bumblebees and entreated: "Come, my friends! Enter the jewel and make it sound!" And so they did.

7 On hearing the sound, the lord of the dead finally consented and said: "Very well, you can take the bones." But he called his servants, those resembling quail, and he ordered them: "Gods, do not allow Quetzalcoatl to depart with the bones. Make sure that he leaves them here, for in all truth, I do greatly appreciate them."

8 But Ce Acatl, who was aware of the plan, thought: "It will not be so; I will take the treasure at once." He said to his Nahual: "My twin, go and tell the deities of the dust that I will leave the bones here."

9 Then the Nahual went, shouting: "I will come to deliver the bones!" At the same time Ce Acatl took the precious bones, wrapped them in a bundle, and went up to the earth. The bones of the woman and the man were mixed together; they were not yet separated.[2]

10 Again the lord called his servants: "Gods, is it possible that Quetzalcoatl has taken the precious bones? Go and find him! In his way make a pit so that he will fall in, then bring me what is mine."

11 The servants did as they were told. They frightened Ce Acatl so that he stumbled and he fell into the pit. The precious bones scattered all over, getting mixed up and broken as they slid. Then the quail took them, biting and gnawing at them.[3]

12 When Ce Acatl came back to his senses, he grieved and told his Nahual: "What am I going to do, my twin? What has happened?" The Nahual answered: "Nothing. Your task went awry. Try it again and let it happen as it will."

13 Then Ce Acatl reprimanded the lord of the dead and said to his servants: "Back, dust birds! Go somewhere else! Do not bother the one who has made himself divine!" Frightened, the quail retreated.

14 After that, he gathered the bones and put them together, but he muddled the job; they were wrongly placed and splintered. It didn't go well. Ce Acatl lamented, saying:

15 "Oh, you quail, makers of ruin! What have you done with this bundle of bones in striking it, breaking it, and splintering it? Here, I am going to fix them, put them in order, adjust them. I am the priest, the one who came down to the underworld and will ascend from the nine depths."

16 Then he asked the gods from heaven for help, saying: "Come my father, Tezcatlipoca! Show me the way so that I, the priest, will not offend you. And you spirits that sustain the earth, the ones that go in the four directions and are the support of heaven, come and help me.

17 "I have come here with your permission. You guided my steps to this dark place. Let me, the son of Ometeotl, finish my task.

18 "And you, jeweled mountains, fringed with turquoise, on whose sides I have stopped and rested more than once, have compassion for these bones, for the whole thing is done, the end has come. Come to help me, father and mother, land and water, starry sky, and you, father of lightning, god that once was an ill man. You offered yourself in sacrifice, and today you share your jades."[4]

19 On hearing his call, the gods came to escort him as he ascended to heaven. When he arrived there, the old mother took the bones and murmured: "So much damage these birds of fear have caused! Affliction, affliction! Now we will fix it."

20 She put the bones in a mill and milled them. Then she poured corn flour in a precious earthenware bowl and kneaded it with the dust from the bones. Ce Acatl cut his virile member and bled over the dough. After that the five gods—Tlaloc, Huictlolinqui, Teponquizqui, Tlallamanac, and Tzontemoc[5]—also came to bleed themselves.

21 Then Xolotl, the Nahual, modeled human figures from the paste, and he nourished them, pouring into their mouth juice from young maize. Then he announced, "They have been born, oh gods, the deserving ones, the new dwellers! This has been possible because of our sacrifice."

22 The old ones narrate that during four more days he wandered around the upper regions where he went to replenish himself with lightning. On the eighth day he came out in the shape of the star called Quetzalcoatl, and he manifested himself at dawn and at dusk. They say that only then did he come to the throne as a lord.

❈ Sources for this chapter: *Anales de Cuautitlán* and *Códice Florentino*.

---

1. The lord of the dead asks him to blow, which is impossible because Ce Acatl doesn't have a body anymore. In asking Ce Acatl to go around his circle four times, he alludes to the four cyclic comings of Quetzalcoatl until Naxcitl, the Fourth Step. He is asking Ce Acatl to demonstrate his messianic state.
2. This alludes to the original androgynous beings.
3. This episode is an explanation of why the newly created humans came to be imperfect and separate genders.
4. He is referring to Nanahuatzin, a Quetzalcoatl before Ce Acatl, who was worshiped in the Teotihuacan culture.
5. These are Quetzalcoatl's five titles, corresponding to each of his theoretical comings. Respectively, they mean: "lord of the earth," "penitent," "solar musician," "star maker," and "cutter of heads."

CHAPTER FOURTEEN

ON THE COAST OF THE PANUCO

1 After four years, he returned. He was walking like a god on the coast of the Panuco.[1] Some travelers recognized him and proclaimers spread the word. On hearing it, many were confused and asked themselves: "Could it be that someone can come back from among the dead? Has something like this ever happened before? Might this be a trick from those evil ones?"

2 Some officials were sent to meet him, but knowing their doubts, he appeared to them on their way and said to them: "Do not doubt, my friends! It is I, Quetzalcoatl the priest, the traveler from the region of the dead! Recognize me! I am the precursor, the one who goes ahead of men to search for the seed there where there are many bones.

3 "I am the warrior, the one who makes his way from heaven. Not in vain I wore the badge of gold. Because of me the sun is moving. I have returned to open my hand, I, dweller in the region of the wings, the lone walker. I fought on the wall of the field of rigor. There I raised my cry, there I earned my name: Defender of Man.

4 "My enemies allied themselves to make war on me, despicable men came against me. Many harms they caused me, those birds of dust. They broke me, they tore me, they stained my precious vessel. Look! My white flag shook the dust, swirled the earth, there in the cavern of penitence."

5 So he said, and then he vanished from sight. The messengers were astonished, then quickly went back to the camp to tell what happened.

> ❈ Sources for this chapter: *Romances de los señores de la Nueva España* and *Historia de las indias.*

1. A river in the state of Veracruz.

CHAPTER FIFTEEN

WITH THE PAGES

1 The pages didn't want to hear the news. They were suspicious that Tezcatlipoca's spirit was walking among them. They asked themselves: "Who is he who comes to perturb us? On whose authority has he taken that name? We saw his body in the bonfire. Didn't he say, *Not twice one lives on earth?*"

2 Among them, one in particular cautioned the others: "Oh priests, do not allow yourselves to be confused. See, the people grow impatient; our voice is not heard. Very soon there will be no memory of the penitent. It is not the Lord but the demon himself who comes to divide us. We must do something."

3 Promptly they decided to send someone to apprehend him. But Ce Acatl, knowing their thoughts, went to the assembly of priests and asked: "Who is the one who is murmuring words of mistrust against me? It is I, the priest, the lord of transformations! I have come back, I have remade myself. I reached true life. Here I am!

4 "My own mother of the sun cloth inspired in me a new and immortal breath. Who could now rise against me? To the dark immensity of the waters I threw my own darkness, I, the penitent, the lord of transformation. I am coming from conquering my destiny!

5 "I have gone to rest in the nine worlds above us. There in the old woman's place my necklace was opened, my garland of feathers was untied. The serpent was crushed! She wanted to break the small mirror, the magical reflection. She was condemned forever to the abyss of perdition!

6 "Look at me, my friends: I am the light; I am the dragon.[1] I know the old man and the old woman. I have lived in the world of the dead and with the ones who never die. I am a mediator! I have come to destroy the one who bites through his four extremities, to sleep the dream, and to gag death. What god or what power will now be capable of throwing me into the dust?"

7 He then invoked his mother so they would recognize him: "Come, you, my mother, with your skirt of stars! Cast your sight over these priests so that they can see, for they are hoping for your light in the house of illumination." So he said.

8 When they heard him, the pages retreated and covered their faces, and the ones who had planned to apprehend him were left speechless and instead worshiped him. Great fear overwhelmed all of them, but he comforted them, saying: "Do not fear! Rejoice, my friends; recognize me!"

9 They happily ran to meet him and surrounded him. "You see, I am back. I have returned from the heart of the sea, from beyond where the horizon stains itself with the inks of dawn. Weren't you expecting it? I am the quetzal! I have come, flying. I have come a difficult passage, from beyond, from the Great War.

10 "When I departed from Tula, my face was somber; my sides were thin and my steps hesitant. I longed to become a flower, and was a bloodied rabbit! I didn't know it, my friends, but in the temple of flames it was revealed to me! I didn't understand it, but in the house of the children, in the garden of the sucklings, it was revealed to me!

11 "After so much traveling, at last I saw a pass, beyond, in the sea's bosom, at the curved edge of the world where the sands scatter without shape. I myself burned this coffer of jades and was reborn. Now look at me: I am the rich owner of jewels, of songs, of broad feathers. I know jades through my own experience!

12 "My heart has come to be perfect. Alone, in the midst of infinite colors, my heart lives. I have received the power of the water ring. I must live eternally in art on this earth!"

13 Drunk with these words, Macuilxochitl exclaimed: "It is you, our leader, bewitching prince! It is truly you, lord of life, protector of all growth! And we gave you only tribulations!" This he said sadly, referring to the doubts with which they had received him.

14 But he responded to Macuilxochitl with affection: "Only the ones who don't know me offend me. You, however, are my parents, my brothers, my beloved priests. You, my brothers, my helpers, will also go, in a turquoise vessel, to the glory of the lord of the infinite currents."

15 Then Matlaxochitl asked him: "Lord, what should we do to be with you, there where you live? How can we reach a face, a heart? How can we sing your chant?"

16 He answered him: "Only the one who comes to be himself, as I, god of dawn and owner of light have done, will be able to sing my chant. Only he will be the one who may mask his face at will. Do not fear, my friends; I am the dragon; I am the light. I send my rays to all created beings, and to those in the paradise of the waters. And the one whom I want, I take and make him mine.

17 "I have arrived at the crossroads of all roads. I have made myself creator, sustainer, and life. What else should I look for? Whom should I follow? I, the provider of the kingdom of the waters, from God I make rain. I, the provider, give to the one who provides for you. Could there be something difficult for me to accomplish? I wish, my friends, that you would also sing my chant.

18 "Therefore, go everywhere, establish yourselves even on the mountain of darkness! With the music of clouds you will spread Ometeotl's glory. Go everywhere; do not fear. My voice will be heard eternally among you, explaining the word of truth."

> Sources for this chapter: *Romances de los señores de la Nueva España; Tratado de las idolatrías;* and *Chilam Balam, libro de los libros.*

1. Cipactonal, "dragon of light," is one title for Quetzalcoatl as a lord of time.

CHAPTER SIXTEEN

THE ORDAINING

1 After these words, he called to his side four young Cholutecs for whom he felt a special love. He commended them to remember all that they had seen and heard, and he asked them to scatter themselves all over the country and be his witnesses before the peoples of the earth.

2 He ordered them to divide the earth into four parts, leaving the city of Cholula as a fifth part and central region; and then he told each one to look after one of the parts, helping the destitute there, facing dictators, and defending the cult of peace.[1] And he asked them to spread the news of his return.

3 He also gave them authority to take priestly power in his name, not as lords who claim the ownership of a kingdom, but rather as servants, as debtors, as someone who takes something on loan until it's time to give it back.

4 He told them: "You will live together under the elders' guidance, sharing your sustenance without accumulating riches. You will watch over and pass on the honors you receive. With all your heart you will take care that the doctrine you received and the Toltec way of life expand. You will keep order in your communities, suppressing all that is lax and preserving virtuosity.

5 "Further, I give you power to create marvelous things, and through it you will make yourselves deserving of the Toltec name, which you will pass on. You will travel through valleys and over mountains, investigating everything in life and finding worthy customs and history and enlightened beliefs. Bring them to your communities and share them with everyone, for then you will reach perfection in the Toltec way.

6 "Even more, wherever you go, ask for the history of the place, understanding the dark side of the people there and helping out in their rituals and traditions only as long as they are favorable to your nature as Toltecs. But beware of human sacrifices and idolatry, and carefully protect yourselves from them!

7 "In your routines study the sacred books, for they are Ometeotl's voice. Talk daily with your heart; keep vigil at night; practice the arts and professions. And above all things, rigorously respect these precepts: Ihiotzin, Icatzin, and Teomania.[2]

8 "Never miss the nightly bath, and never pass a razor over your head. Sleep and eat just a little, and speak only when necessary. Be moderate in your manners and sober in your dress. Do not wear jewels or sumptuous clothing, but only a stone or wooden necklace. Sing praises until dawn and do not forget penitence.

9 "Work sowing the land, so that you will not be a burden to people; feed the needy, the poor, the anchorites, and the ill; and help at all times widows and orphans.

10 "And here is how you will elect your chiefs: Those among you who are leaders will work double shift. The most humble among you will represent you. The one of most noble birth will be a servant. And there will be no reward for these services.

11 "Only the one with a pure heart, a good heart, a firm, man's heart, only the one with Ometeotl in his heart and who is wise in the things of God will represent you. His name is not important, nor his birth, even if his origin is miserable, even if his father and mother are poor among the poor. You will not pay attention to his lineage, but rather to his way of living.

12 "If you find someone who leads a good life, with perfect habits, practices, and doctrines—one who is sober and a keeper of the precepts; virtuous, humble and peaceful; considerate, sane, compassionate, friendly to all; devoted, God-fearing, and clear—then he is the one you will choose as a supreme priest with the title of Quetzalcoatl. This one will serve you as a guide; he will carry you on his back and will govern you.

13 "Such a guide will tell you how to worship Ometeotl; he will make the offerings and the smudging vessel. His duties will be making speeches, busying himself night and day with incense, preparing the thorns for penitence, watching and calculating the movements and order in the sky and the division of the night, and he will not sleep to keep you awake.

14 "He will read and sing; he will turn noisily the pages of the codices; he will have the black and red inks and the glyphs to raise you, to guide you, to show you the way. He will also order the fall of the year, the accounting of the destinies and the days, and the twentieths. He will talk about the gods. These are the reasons you will call him Quetzalcoatl.

15 "When men or women want to join you because of your good example, gladly accept them. You can receive everyone without distinction, on the condition that they accept these restrictions: They should remain chaste, renounce family ties, and commit themselves to communal work; they should be temperate and practice fasting; they should love to study; they should accept admonishment with humility, and they should subjugate their bodies and have no fear of penitence.

16 "These are the people you will not admit: children, slaves, those lacking sound judgment; those with grave physical problems; those who have addictions, and those who lack love of God.[3]

17 "To determine the sincerity of those who want to follow you, you will ask of them to be alone for four years in the mountains, feeding themselves from roots and wild fruits, so that they can assess their intention.[4] And if even after that, that man or woman persists in joining you, you will take them and lead them before the image of our mother, the goddess of the waters, or before a creek or a lake in the woods, and you will make an invocation as follows:

18 "I take this water from your hands, Lady, to wash this being that before you has come to wash the stain inherited from his parents. The water will take and disperse the stain and the guilt. And you, Lady, be so kind as to purify this heart and this life that I place in your hands. For only you are favored with the gift to cleanse all stains from before the beginning of the world."[5] And so speaking, pour water over the head of the solicitant and thereby admit him into the community.

19 "And if one of those whom you have admitted continues sinning, do not reject him, but allow him to come and confess to the elders. And an elder will tell him:

20 "'You, as a precious and purified thing, were engendered again by your father and mother, Quetzalcoatl. Out of your own free will you have turned to sullying yourself. Confess now, open up and manifest yourself before your lord. He is a protector, he is understanding.'

21 "Do not undervalue this advice because, in truth, confessing one's guilt will make us enter the bridge of mercy. It is like the clear water that Ometeotl uses to purify our soul and make us to be born anew, to live again. He gives us new light and new sun, and makes us bloom and shine with beams of a new life from our mother, the womb in which we were nurtured.

22 "And when he confesses his sins, impose upon him penitence and tell him: 'Now you will work one year or two, sweeping the patio of the house of God at dawn. Now you will pierce your body with agave thorns; you will pierce your lips, ears, arms, legs, or virile member according to your sin, whether it is from talking, hearing, doing, or craving. Now you will visit the sanctuaries naked, in the cold of the night; you will sacrifice your words, your breath, and your glances. Now you will deliver yourself to the river, wherever it wants to take you.'

23 "And these will be the sins that you will watch out for: harmful or injurious words with which you affront people; ungratefulness for Ometeotl's favors; the inhumanity that you have shown by not making offerings for some of the other goods that your God has given you; withholding the communication of that which has been communicated to you;[6] faults against the divine precepts or against the customs of the community; adultery; deceit; and sleep."

✸ Sources for this chapter: *Historia de las indias; Códice Florentino;* and *Memoriales.*

---

1. This theopolitical order was ideologically respected until the Aztecs came to power. Quetzalcoatl's bloodless religion, however, was the only one that remained pure in the Cholula region.
2. These translate as "reverential breathing," "reverential posture," and "meditation on the divine things."

3. Children and slaves were excluded from monastic communities because they had no capacity (in the case of the former) and no right (in the case of the latter) to make decisions. People with physical handicaps could not withstand the rigor of the initiations. With time, these precepts were revoked, and the monasteries came to be full of children.

4. This practice was not as hard as it seems, for Indo-American societies were educated to assist the anchorites.

5. In this theology, the origin of the human being is immaculate; only its accidental connection with the world of shapes produces an impression of sin.

6. This refers to passing on Ce Acatl's message.

CHAPTER SEVENTEEN

THE COMMANDMENTS

1 After these words Quetzalcoatl concluded his speech, saying: "And this is my final word, that which will identify you as my followers and friends, that which will make you true Toltecs, authentic Mace-huals, that which you must follow and share, for it is chosen food.

2 "I wish to entrust to you only three commandments: The first is that you try with all eagerness to make friends with the one who is everywhere in everyone at each moment, for he is night and wind and Lord of the intimate living.

3 "Beware that through your engagement in this task you do not become arrogant, anxious, or cowardly, but rather remain humble at heart, laying all your hopes in Ometeotl and daring to sustain his prescriptions.

4 "The second thing that you must remember is to be at peace with all men; do not offend anyone; respect everyone. Do not shame another man for any reason. Be calm; let others say of you whatever they will. Be quiet and do not respond, even if they attack you. That is how you will show your virile condition and your nobility, and everyone will know that you are a trustworthy representative of me. All of this is accomplished by actively training yourselves in the practice of peace.

5 "And the third thing that I ask of you is this: Don't waste the time that Ometeotl has given you on this earth. Busy yourselves night and day with that which is good. Do not despise time, for you do not know if you will live again or if you will recognize your own faces there. Make the best of your lives.

6 "Enough of this. This was my mission. From now on, do as you please. Every man will acquire excellence for himself and will conquer life."

7 That is how he finished his exhortation. And the disciples took his words to their hearts, to repeat them later among all their friends.

Sources for this chapter: *Huehuetlahtolli de Padre Olmos* and *Suma indiana.*

CHAPTER EIGHTEEN

THE PROPHECY

1 After that he asked them to summon everyone to the edge of the sea so that he could deliver his blessings and his promise. Quickly all of the people gathered. He then went to a nearby rock, climbed it, and announced to the multitude the words of his prophecy. And these were his words:

2 "Listen to me, brothers: I, Quetzalcoatl, colored with blood of serpents, have been born anew. I have become a self-made man in battle, and that is how I came to be my own father. I have come to know destiny's cycles, there where the waters expand and time stops. I only came to prepare a way.

3 "Now I must go. But do not be afraid; I am not going forever. You will hear my voice eternally; my song will always return. Do not cry for the bygone prince. I have left you my face, my words, my jewels. Cheer up!

4 "A new day is coming, the magnificent day of radiant beauty when I must return to myself. Then you will see me! You brothers will understand the divine reasons. I will raise my harvest and gather what I have sowed. The evil animal will forever disappear, and you will be able to walk in peace.

5 "The golden doors will open, and the peoples of earth will come in matrimony to the temple of the four directions, where you will be asked that you not take off your sandals. And the symbol of unity will manifest itself in an erected tree. When this comes to be, the world will see it. It will be Ometeotl's dawn.

6 "The power of kindness will now come to you, to enliven you and to take away all fear from the world, power of unity, power from the heart of heaven, the one who, upon receiving us, receives only his proper self. Give devotion to truth; believe in its power! Enliven the light in your hearts, oh brothers! The world will rise for those who understand.

7 "At the distance of a shout, at the distance of a day's journey, your man already waits, your elder brother, the green jade one, the bearded one with a pilgrim's staff: Tlahuizcalpantecuhtli. Time is growing closer; the hour is coming. The humanity of the new sun has been born. See its sign now! Raise the pole![1]

> 🏵 Sources for this chapter: *Chilam Balam, libro de los libros* and *Cantares de los señores de la Nueva España.*

1. The Christian chroniclers wanted to see in this "erected tree" a prophecy of the Christian cross, but even though it is shaped as a cross, it is more than that. It signifies the tree of origin. For the Nahuas it represented the axis of the world, the spinal column, and the illumination.

CHAPTER NINETEEN

THE RAFT OF SERPENTS

1 He then took his mantle of serpents and threw it into the water. It floated on the sea like a raft; it did not sink. He then sailed away from the shore upon it. And as he departed, Ce Acatl blessed his people with these words:

2 "May the creator of men, the connoisseur of men, look upon every one of you with love! May all of you be happy and may you take all that I gave you as food from my lips and mouth! May the earth remain forever and the mountains remain standing! May the flowers of roasted corn and the perfumed flowers of cacao be scattered all over the world! Let the earth remain forever!"

3 The raft of serpents traveled far over the waters of the sea, toward the eastern horizon. And the elders relate that he entered into heaven. This happened in the year of Ce Acatl, in the year of his birth. And the knowledgeable elders say that Quetzalcoatl truly lives; he did not die, he will return once again; he will come back to be king.

Sources for this chapter: *Cantares de los señores de la Nueva España; Memorial Breve;* and *Códice Vatacino A.*

CHAPTER TWENTY

THE END OF
THE TOLTECS

1 Soon the news of his return from the region of the dead reached the city of Tula. There the Toltecs received it with great joy. The memory of his glory was still alive among them, and the love for the prince and penitent was not extinguished.

2 Following Tula's example, other cities also welcomed Ce Acatl's messengers, and all, in concert with Cholula's priests, established alliances for the defense of Toltecayotl.[1]

3 All this filled Tezcatlipoca and his partisans with rancor. He visited all the enemies of the kingdom, inciting them to lay siege to it. He also went into the Toltec ranks. From one side to the other he went, inciting both of them. Many bittter people joined in.

4 At last he moved against Tula, bringing with him a great army that mocked the city's inhabitants and desecrated the sanctuaries. The Toltecs, who were committed to peace and who for many generations did not indulge in the arts of war, saw themselves at a great disadvantage and were therefore defeated. They all fell: old men, young men, children, and women; no one was spared.

5 Those who survived ran away toward the region of Xicco. They left abandoned temples and palaces. And all of this fulfilled the prophecy: "Oh Tula, center of the earth! You will be left an orphan."

6 The king Huemac fled with the surviving people and established his camp in Xicco where he tried to present some kind of resistance. There his woman, named Cuauhnehec, gave birth. For this reason he named the place after her. Tezcatlipoca pursued them all the way to this place.

7 Huemac's followers had brought with them a serpent that they venerated and that demanded a human victim. Seeing themselves in a desperate situation, they agreed to sacrifice a man for her. Huemac, on learning of this abomination, removed himself from them and retired to a cave on the way to Chapultepec. There he cried sadly and sang a song:

8 "I am grieved today with lamentable luck. In the fields lay broken arrows, scattered heads of hair, and roofless houses with reddened walls. In the plazas and the streets worms are circulating and the walls are splashed with brains.

9 "The water is red, like ink, and when we drink it, it is as if we are drinking saltpeter. When we search for food we strike the adobe walls, and our inheritance is a net of holes. We wanted to shelter ourselves under shields, but not even shields can sustain us in our loneliness!

10 "Here I am, running through life. I have eaten sticks of *eryngo*[2] to arrive here. I have chewed saltpeter gum, adobe stones, lizards, mice, worms, dust. All of this has happened to us. I have seen it."

11 Then, after passing a rope over the tree at the mouth of the cave, he took his life. Huemac suffered a great deal for the end of his people. When he saw that no one followed him because they had already come to their end, the king committed suicide.

12 Huemac's newborn son, the prince Pochotl, whom Cuauhnehec gave birth to, escaped with his nurse toward the Nonoalco deserts.

> ▒ Sources for this chapter: *Relaciones históricas* and *Historia general de las cosas de la Nueva España.*

1. The Toltequity.
2. Eryngo is a plant with spiny leaves and dense clusters of small, bluish flowers. It was formerly considered an aphrodisiac.

CHAPTER TWENTY-ONE
THE MESQUITE

1 The few Toltecs who were capable of escaping with their lives scattered themselves throughout the mountains and swamps. Their princes and artisans hid in the courts of the kingdoms where they were received. Tezcatlipoca stopped chasing them.

2 The total number of dead among the Toltecs was 3,200,000. This marked the end of Tula and its kingdom. The city was never again inhabited.

3 But the sorcerer, gathering all his partisans around a mesquite tree, climbed the tree and said: "Stop, friends! Let the Toltecs scatter! You, my devotees, will not scatter!"

4 After that he proclaimed them a nation and gave them laws. He named thirteen lords over them and exhorted them to remember their duties, saying: "Never become vain, my friends. Always remember how many hardships we endured in Tula until we reached our goals. Proceed with humility and sacrifice.

5 "You, Itztecólotl, do not become proud. If you become arrogant like the Toltecs, I will destroy you. I will do as I did to Maxtla, the corporal. Remember his two daughters whom he kept in a coffer like precious stones? I made them give birth to twins, to two obnoxious beasts."

6 After lecturing them in this way, he led them to the valley of Xaltocan in order to leave the Toltec kingdom uninhabited. And that, finally, is how Hueman's prophecy came to be.

Source for this chapter: *Relaciones históricas*.

BIBLIOGRAPHY

This story was reconstructed from biographical and philosophical texts contained in the following sources.

Alcalá, Jerónimo de. *La relación de michoacán*. SEP, 1988.

Anales de Cuautitlán. Universidad Nacional Autónoma de Mexico, 1945.

Anales de los Cakchikeles (Xil). Universidad Nacional Autónoma de Mexico, 1993.

Cantares de Dzitbalche, Universidad Nacinal Autónoma de Mexico, 1948.

Cantares de los Mexicanos.

Cantares de los señores de la Nueva España. Universidad Nacional Autónoma de Mexico, 1963.

Chilam Balam de Chumayel. SEP, 1985.

Chilam Balam de Tuzik. Grupo Dzibil, 1996.

Chilam Balam, libro de los libros. Dante, 1989.

Chimalpahin, Don Francisco de San Aton Munon. *Memorial Breve*. Universidad Nacional
Autónoma de Mexico, 1991.

Códice Aubin. Sec. Fomento, 1902.

Códice Chimalpopoca. Universidad nacional Autónoma de Mexico, 1945.

Códice Vatacino A. Biblioteca Vatacino, 1900.

Huehuetlahtolli de Padre Olmos. Frank Díaz, 1995.

Durán, Diego. *Historia de las indias*. Escalante, 1980

Hernandez, Francisco. *Antiguedades de los indios*. Porrúa, 1964.

Ixtlixochitl, Alba. *Relaciones históricas*. Sec. Fomento, 1892.

Landa, Diego. *Descripcion de las cosas de Yucatan*. Universidad Nacional Autónoma de Mexico.

Las Casa, Bartolomé. *Los indios de México y Nueva España*. Porrúa, 1982.

Leyenda de los soles. Universidad Nacional Autónoma de Mexico, 1945

Leyenda del Tepozteco. Cook, 1989.

López de Gómara. *Historia de la Nueva España*. Iberia, 1954.

Mártir de Angeleria, Pedro. *Decadas del Nuevo Mundo*. Porrúa, 1964

Motolinía, Toribio Benavente. *Memoriales*. Universidad Nacional Autónoma de Mexico, 1994.

Popol Vuh. FCE, 1973.

Romances de los señores de la Nueva España. Universidad Nacional Autónoma de Mexico, 1963.

Ruiz de Alarcón, H. *Tratado de las ilolatrías*. Fuente Cultural, 1953.

Sahagún, Bernardino de. *Historia general de las cosas de la Nueva España*. Alianza Editorial, 1988.

———. *Suma indiana*. Universidad Nacional Autónoma de Mexico, 1943.

———. *Códice Florentino*. Troncoso, 1905.

Teogonía e historia de los Mexicanos. Porrúa, 1979.

Tezozomoc, Fernando Alvarado. *Relaciones I*. Editorial Leyenda, 1944.

FOR FURTHER INFORMATION ON QUETZALCOATL AND THE TOLTECS, CONTACT:

The Society for Quetzalcoatl Knowledge

Calle Nube 13, San Geronimo, México DF

CP 10000

Tel. 5-668-2609

Fax. 5-568-9781

E-mail: ssoll@hotmail.com.mx

BOOKS OF RELATED INTEREST

The Teachings of Don Carlos
Practical Applications of the Works of Carlos Castaneda
by Victor Sanchez

The Toltec Path of Recapitulation
Healing Your Past to Free Your Soul
by Victor Sanchez

Toltecs of the New Millennium
by Victor Sanchez

Don Juan and the Art of Sexual Energy
The Rainbow Serpent of the Toltecs
by Merilyn Tunneshende

Don Juan and the Power of Medicine Dreaming
A Nagual Woman's Journey of Healing
by Merilyn Tunneshende

Mastery of Awareness
Living the Agreements
by Doña Bernadette Vigil with Arlene Broska, Ph.D.

Primal Awareness
*A True Story of Survival, Transformation, and Awakening
with the Rarámuri Shamans of Mexico*
by Don Trent Jacobs

Return of the Children of Light
Incan and Mayan Prophecies for a New World
by Judith Bluestone Polich

Inner Traditions • Bear & Company
P.O. Box 388
Rochester, VT 05767
1-800-246-8648
www.InnerTraditions.com

Or contact your local bookseller